Look Deep Inside

*A True Inspiring Story About
Knowing Who We Really Are*

JANE DIMITROVSKI

BALBOA.PRESS
A DIVISION OF HAY HOUSE

Balboa Press books may be ordered through booksellers or by contacting:

Balboa Press
A Division of Hay House
1663 Liberty Drive
Bloomington, IN 47403
www.balboapress.com
844-682-1282

Because of the dynamic nature of the Internet, any web addresses or links contained in this book may have changed since publication and may no longer be valid. The views expressed in this work are solely those of the author and do not necessarily reflect the views of the publisher, and the publisher hereby disclaims any responsibility for them.

The author of this book does not dispense medical advice or prescribe the use of any technique as a form of treatment for physical, emotional, or medical problems without the advice of a physician, either directly or indirectly. The intent of the author is only to offer information of a general nature to help you in your quest for emotional and spiritual well-being. In the event you use any of the information in this book for yourself, which is your constitutional right, the author and the publisher assume no responsibility for your actions.

Print information available on the last page.

ISBN: 978-1-9822-6895-4 (sc)
ISBN: 978-1-9822-6896-1 (e)

Balboa Press rev. date: 05/28/2021

DEDICATED TO MY PARENTS, WHO GAVE ME
MORE THAN I COULD UNDERSTAND

I AM NOT WHO YOU THINK I AM, I AM NOT
WHO I THINK I AM, I AM WHO I THINK YOU
THINK I AM.

- THOMAS COOLEY

Contents

Introduction

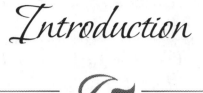

This incredible true story about the realization of who we really are was created in a time of total mental chaos in which we find ourselves very often – but we don't speak about that openly because we think everybody will think that we are crazy.

No, we are not crazy.

No, you are not crazy.

That is only the ego trying to make us look like we are crazy.

No, we are not the ego mind.

We are more than that.

Even I had strong pressure from my Ego mind,

I was still following the God feeling inside me and the calling to write and share my experience with all of you and now I feel so relieved when my book is already out there, where actually it belongs, in public. Everybody has the right to know that we can make our dreams come true, that we are born with true power within. We just need to be brave enough and not give up. Even when our ego mind dominates us, we must make a clear distinction from it, and know that it is not our true self.

I start this book with small talk between me and my higher self and I leave you the choice to believe in that or not. It's all in your imagination, my lovely.

And then I divided this book into the three most important parts.

The first one I called, "The way I found my true Self", where I share with you my own journey - how I found HIM, GOD, in the most unexpected place that you can ever imagine, deep inside me, only by following the signs, signs put there by HIM, and I am sharing also in this first part of my Book my interesting journey of how I found my soulmate to.

In the second part I speak about how changing our point of view, first of ourselves and then of everything around us, and especially of that which has happened to us until this point in our lives, can impact our lives in a positive way and make us realize that everything in our lives happens for a reason. That's why I called this part,

"From another point of view."

I called the third part, "Believe and Receive", because when we find out who we really are, and by choosing consciously to have another point of view or another way of thinking about ourselves and about others, it only remains for us to believe that everything that we ever wished and dreamed for in our lives is on its way to us, and that we just need to be ready to receive it.

To receive everything that belongs to us, and that is happiness, joy, health and wealth. In fact, we are already born with all this, the only problem is, we have already forgotten it. This book is only a reminder that our true power is within, deep inside, in ourselves.

That's why you need to LOOK DEEP INSIDE and surrender to the feeling of oneness, my lovely.

Sit comfortably and enjoy it.

With Love,
your JD 🙏

God, please open the door…

I am knocking God, please open the door.

Who are you?

I am one of your children. I was looking for you everywhere: in church, but you were not there, in the Bible, but you were not there, in the sky, but you were not there either. And then I felt something in the middle of my chest and then I knew you are here, inside, in me!

So please God, open the door, I want to know more about you.

Why do you want to know more about me, my son? You already know everything you are supposed to know.

How do you mean that God?

Do you believe in God?

Of course.

And you believe that with God all things are possible?

Yes, I believe!

And you have this feeling inside, within you, that I am Here, in you?

Yes, I do.

Then you are also God, you are also part of me and I am part of you, we are not separate and you can make everything possible for yourself.

That's why belief in yourself is belief in me, God.

And belief in God is belief in yourself.

Very simple, isn't it?

And when you believe that you can make all things possible for yourself, then and only then will these things happen to you.

Thank you, God, but I had to admit it wasn't always this way.

I had doubts about myself and sometimes about you too.

That's the path that you are supposed to walk, my son.

And the best part is that this Feeling of Oneness with you is always with me, when I am happy, when I am sad, when I am angry, when I have a job, when I don't have a job, with money, without money, this feeling Is always here!

But, dear God, why did you give me this Feeling of Oneness with you?

Am I the only one who has this feeling?

Please say yes.

That's very funny.

But it's not true my son, everybody has this feeling inside them.

But everybody is looking for help or a solution for their problems outside of themselves, in the world around them, but when you look inside, deep inside yourself, there is a whole world inside and a solution for every problem.

As I said, I didn't give it only to you, my son, this feeling was here all the time inside you, and in everybody else too, but now you have recognized it!

Do you know why?

No.

You wanted to help, didn't you?

You have asked me 100 times a day,

How can I help, God?

What is my calling?

How can I serve you?

My universe?

My people?

How can I make a difference?

How can I make the world a better place?

Are these your questions?

Yes God, those are my questions!

I know all your wishes, my son.

Here is your chance, share your wisdom with the world, the experience that you had, your knowledge about me, about you, about the Oneness of all beings!

I will, God, I will.

I asked you these questions and more, such as what is my purpose in this world.

Is it only to work in jobs that I don't love only to pay my bills and to wait to die, without leaving a trace that I was once alive and that I once walked this Earth, or is there is something more for me, some greater purpose, to become recognized by helping others and not to be always seen as the one who needs help?

That is what I meant when I said to you that you already know everything that you are supposed to know. If you want to help, then talk about it, share your experience with the world.

I will God, I will,

I know it won't be easy, I'm a little scared because I have been dominated all my life by my EGO mind and it is trying even now, every minute, to pull me back with its negative thoughts that it won't work out, that I will fail, but I know now that this is its game, just to make me scared, and your presence in my chest says to me every single minute, "Don't be afraid, Jane, do it, I am with you, I always was, and I always will be with you. Just do it!"

By the way, what can I lose, really?

I am a graduate of Philosophy who is working as a security guard to pay the bills and the rent and to buy one toy for each of my three beautiful kids, and I am writing my first book about my extraordinary experiences in the job on my night shifts, because at home it is a bit difficult with three small angels. So what can I lose, my lovely?

Nothing! And I don't want to keep my mouth closed anymore, I don't want to keep this experience only for myself, I want to share it with the world.

I am ready to speak to the world about how I found you, GOD, in a place where most people are not used to looking for you, in ourselves. To be honest with you, I wasn't either, but I did, and I am very happy about that.

And if I can with my Book to help ten other people to find you in themselves, and become better persons, colleagues, fathers, husbands or sons, my mission will have been accomplished.

Now let's go!

I suppose I have to start with my early beginnings, and how I always followed my heart, and how that ended with finding my soulmate and how, two years ago, I found my peace, my strength, my inspiration. I found HIM, deep inside me!

This true story may inspire you to also begin to follow your heart and to look deep inside yourself. Believe me, no gold, no wealth in the whole world can be compared with this feeling.

Sit comfortably and enjoy it.

With love,

your JD🙏

The Way I Found My True Self

Mama, please can you take him back to the hospital and get another baby who doesn't cry so much?

Very funny but I can't Honey, this is your brother, your little brother, and we love him so much even though he cries day and night.

Yes, that was me.

Born as a second child in a small town where there was only one hospital at that time (and it's still the same today), and there was already resentment from my best friend, my sister, from the very beginning.☺

In my heart she was and she will always be my best friend.☺

From the stories that I have heard about myself in my first five years until I became aware of my existence, I was a child who was in charge of keeping the whole house awake. At that time my Dad was working as a book salesman in another country and my Mom was alone at home with me and my older sister.

Maybe that's why I took on my Dad's role and was yelling all day and night just to show who's the boss in the house.☺

According to my Mom's stories, that was a very hard period of her life.

She alone with two small children, she had a full-time job, and my Dad's parents were also in the same house.

Mom, I can only imagine how that could have been.☹

She had to do almost everything alone at that time, to take me to kindergarten, to look after me, to take care of my sister, to go to work. And she had already had a very hard childhood, especially with her parents.

Thanks Mom♥

I had a beautiful relationship with her.

With my Dad it was not so good, unfortunately, but from this point of view today, he did the best he could as a parent.

Unfortunately, they had something in common.

They were never satisfied with us as children, especially with me, (at least I thought that they were never satisfied with me).

After that period of my life where I showed my Mom and my sister that life is too short to waste time on sleeping, came the most challenging time for a child, the time to go to school.

To be honest with you, I cannot remember my first day at school and who took me there, and what it was like, but I certainly know how my time at school ended, with great relief, especially for my Mom, because she spent more time in my school than I did. I wasn't a very quiet and good kid - I mean only in school. ☺

Like most other kids, I didn't know what I wanted to be when I was grown up, but I certainly knew what I definitely *did* want, and like most other kids, that was attention.

I think that was because everything I did at home and at school was seemingly not good enough.

Apart from all the stupid things that I did at school to attract attention to myself, I was a very active and a very talented child, especially at sports.

Because my parents didn't know what to do with all the energy that I had, they wanted me to do Karate. That was the first and last good idea that my parents had. ☺

But not for too long.☺

When I began to do Karate I felt for the first time that this was the way I could beat the fear in me. Fear that I had in me from my early years, fear that I picked up from the environment in which I lived, fear of disappointing my Mom and Dad, of not being a good son, because they were doing everything to provide us with all the things that we had. That's what they told me and my sister. Not only once, but a thousand times.

And that is a mistake that 90% of parents make: by telling their children that they are together only because of them, that they work only because of them, in other words they only live for them! Even if that is the truth, you don't tell it to a child, dear parents.

If you tell that to your children, they'll start to feel responsible for everything that happens to you as a parent, and they will do anything to make you proud as a parent, to give something back, to do something… but unfortunately sometimes not very smart things.

Find a way to find yourself, dear children, to find your passion, especially in the early stages of your life, and make yourself proud of yourself.

To continue my story, to make my parents satisfied I started to do Karate and suddenly I felt great. I thought this was a perfect way to get rid of my fear, until one day I came home and I was so excited that I wanted to show my sister what I had learned in my Karate lessons.

But my Dad was not as excited as I was, and he decide to take me out of my Karate training because I could have hurt my sister.

I was four years younger and smaller than my sister and I could have hurt her?

That was the only way to stop the next Bruce Lee. ☺

Now I can laugh about it, but at the time it might have opened my eyes to the fact that it wouldn't be an easy trip, but I was too young to see that.

Almost the same thing happened with my music lessons.

Some of my school teachers wanted me to go to music school because they thought I might have a talent for music, but first I had to sing a song in class, and then they would decide if I could be accepted by this music school or not.

I was very shy as a kid and I remember I took my Mom with me to my first music class, and that was the moment when I had to show my singing ability. ☺

Because I was too shy, I said to my teacher that I would sing a song, but that first all of the children would have to leave the room.

That was very funny for everybody of course, but not for me, nobody understood me.

Nobody tried to approach me from a different angle. I was just a kid, a very shy kid.

That was the only way the next Mozart could be stopped. ☺

I don't know if I can laugh about it even now after 36 years.

Not supporting a child in the early years of their life can have a massive effect on it. A massive negative effect, of course.

On its self-confidence.

In this case on my self-confidence.

But who cared about such things 25-30 years ago? Building self-confidence? 😐😆Nobody!

Life goes on, my lovely.

But that wasn't the worst thing that happened to me at that time.

First, I got hit by a bus 20 meters away from our home as I was coming back from school, and I was so scared that I would be punished by my parents that I didn't tell them about it.

And then they found out, and guess what happened, my lovely?

I got kicked very hard by them for getting hit by a bus.

At that time, I thought, "What lovely parents I have." ☺

But something else happened, something that I didn't expect as a child.

Something that left a big trace on me,

A trace that I would carry with me a long time after I finished school.

I was in the 6th grade, and we had our first excursion with our sports teacher to another city, and we went to a swimming pool to improve our swimming skills.

And then something terrible happened; something that nobody could have expected.

One of our friends drowned in the pool.

A boy who had his whole life ahead of him. Now he was dead.

We stood all around him speechless, watching how they tried to save his life.

Everybody was crying, and they couldn't save his life.

We went back without our friend.

It was a shock for all of us, nobody could believe that he was no longer with us.

We arrived back in our small town without him.

In a situation like this only one emotion can show up, and that was fear.

It gets control over you, especially when you are child.

Yes, the fear is back now.

As always, over and over again.

On the day of the funeral I was so scared that I was going to see him dead, and I didn't know how I was supposed to react, and while we were waiting near his home I got scared so much that I suddenly turned around and ran back home, but I didn't tell anybody about it. Nobody knew about it except me.

In my school days, and as a teenager too, it was not a problem for me to lie to everybody, I was talented in that too😄. But I couldn't lie to myself.

I had my own problems, like every other teenager, but I never forget that a few years ago I hadn't gone to my friend's funeral, only because of you, fear.

Then I did something that nobody from my family knew about, until today.

I saved money during my school week, money that I was supposed to spend on myself, and I got a taxi every Sunday and went to his grave and

I sat there, begging him to forgive me. I think I did that for almost two years until I felt inside me the peace which meant that I didn't need to do it anymore. He had forgiven me.

Thank you, my friend! 🙏Rest in peace 🙏

After that experience I had a thousand questions in my head.

That was the first time I was confronted with another related fear, the fear of my own death.

We can die?

Just like that?

And what happens then?

Is that it?

I was confused and even scared to ask questions about life, death and fear. As with everything else, I was trying to figure it out by myself. ☺

Even as a teenager I went to church very often and I asked questions, but there were no answers, because even if I got some answers I couldn't understand them at that time.

I really struggled at that time as a teenager: I had my "own" problems, I didn't go to school very regularly, and when I was at school I was making trouble. My parents had their own issues, and on top of that there were all these questions in my head about life, death, fear, and the meaning of our lives. It was total chaos.

At that time my parents had a supermarket and I was helping them; I worked in the store. Most of the time I worked after school, sometimes before I went to school, and sometimes I did a night shift. That was the way (not the only way) my dad punished me when he found out that I hadn't been to school.😂

I was really a very active teenager and I did very stupid things at that time: as I said, some of them only to attract attention to myself, and some of them to show to my friends how brave I was. 😊 I was more scared than a five-year-old boy, but I didn't want to show it.

Thank God He was keeping me from evil all the time.

Today, I think most teenagers also do stupid things when they are with their friends, but as parents we must know our children best and know them as they really are. As parents we must be able to recognize when they have done some stupid thing without telling us about it.

That was not the case with my parents.

They had more than enough problems.

Especially my Dad.

For example, he didn't know a lot about me, he never found out that I used to take his car and that I went with my friends to another city; he didn't know that I stole money from his store because every time I asked him to give me some money he gave me so little that it was only enough to have something to eat (thank God my Mom always gave me some more money for other things). He didn't know that I tried all sorts of different drugs as a teenager. He didn't notice any of that at all.

From my point of view as a parent now, I can say that shouldn't happen, but they had their own problems and they loved us and cared about us in their own way, and they were always there for us. Even when I thought that they were not, they were there for us, always! But I had a rough time as a teenager, and on top of that I had a hundred questions in my head, like every other teenager. Only my questions were a little more complicated.

At the age of 15, I can remember that I began to create my picture of God. A God who was in the sky, of course, a God of whom I was supposed to be afraid, a God who was somewhere out there. I didn't know where, but not in me.

Even as a teenager I prayed to HIM in my own childlike way, but I was afraid of HIM and like most of us I only looked for HIM when I was in trouble.

One night I was with my friends on the beautiful mountain above our hometown where we have one of the most beautiful monasteries in the whole world, and were supposed to stay there for three days. We were drinking some alcohol, we were having fun and everything was ok, but then some stupid ideas arose and all of a sudden I found myself under the open sky, alone, with a lot of negative thoughts that something bad would happen to me, and then I said to myself:

Dear God, you are supposed to be in the sky so you can probably hear me from here, I am high up enough. I am on one of the biggest mountains in our country, please help me, I don't want to get hurt!

I felt better, and I didn't get hurt. He only wanted only to show me that he existed, but not there where I was looking for him, in the sky.

He also knew that I was too young to understand that at that moment.

Everything comes at the right time in our lives, and at that time I wasn't ready for another truth except for this knowing that He was sitting there in the sky and He looked down on us and that we had to be afraid of him and do the "right" things or he would punish us.

I don't think it was a problem that I thought like that as a teenager, because that is what was told to me as child, that I was supposed to be afraid of my God and that he is sitting somewhere and looking at me, and it depends on my behavior whether he will react with some good or bad action. But now I do think it is a problem, because even today, many adults still think this way.

How can you be afraid of something that created you? Can something that breathed life into you be a danger for you?

Like a lot of the things in my life, nobody knew what really happened to me and nobody cared (that was my way of thinking at that time as a teenager: that nobody cares). They did care, for sure, but they didn't know how to show it.

I was the bad boy son, I wasn't very pleasant to our teachers, not so quiet in the classes. There was always trouble with me, and when you are a walking source of trouble nobody cares about your feelings. What they didn't know is that it was only my mask, my defense mechanism to protect myself, because only I knew how vulnerable and scared I was.

That was a really rough period for me. I mean I was the teenager who had to experience all the arguments between his parents in 35m2 of living space. I had my own problems: friends, girls, school. I was involved in a few fights, fights that I never started. I did not fit in even when I tried to fit in, and the worst part was that I felt guilty for everything that happened to us as a family. Even though I wasn't at fault at all as a teenager, I felt guilty.

Especially when something bad happened to us.

For example, I was in a position to see how my Dad was losing his stores because of his irresponsible behavior. And my Mom, she quit her job a long time ago only to work with my Dad in his stores. That's tough, both parents without a job. Overnight.

And what does a teenager do in a situation like that?

Tries to help, of course, without telling his parents about it.

Because I had heard so many times how they did everything to provide us with everything we had and now suddenly they were in trouble, and what did I feel?

First, I felt guilt as I said before, and second, I felt obligated to help somehow, sometimes in a very stupid, naive and dangerous way, but I wanted to help!

Another piece of advice for you, my lovely parents out there: never ever speak about your financial problems around your children. Be aware that your children may think that they are the cause of your problems and that they will try to help, even if you don't ask for it. Please, my dear parents, be aware of what you say, especially around your children.

Let's go back to my plan to help. Thank God he was on my side all the time.

First I thought I would rob a bank, but then I thought that I couldn't do it alone, and if I had told somebody else about what I was planning to do, everyone else could have found out about it. I was living in a small town, and that's why I needed a plan where I could work by myself.

Then I found a guy who was very rich at that time and I got his phone number.

I bought a cell phone card and I called him and told him - imitating another voice - that I was some evil criminal and that he had to put 20,000 German marks in an abandoned truck.

Can you imagine that, my lovely?

But thank God he didn't take me seriously. I think he recognized a teenager's voice on the other end of the line.

And guess what my lovely, whose was this abandoned truck? My Dad's, of course.

Very intelligent move from a teenager, don't you think?

It was not so difficult to find out who had called this guy.

My Mom saved me in that situation. She received a phone call from his wife, who claimed that I was the boy who was responsible for the phone call.

My Mom couldn't believe that I was capable of something like that and she called this guy's wife back and she told her that she was crazy accusing a teenager of doing something like that. That is the bad side of living in a small town.😵

Thanks Mom♥

I just wanted to help.☺

But at the end of the day, something protects us all the time, some power, not only me, but thank God the whole of my family too.

And that's how I knew that something higher exists. I was "lonely" with all my problems, but I was not alone, and I kept looking for the answer in church, in our beautiful monastery, even as a young teenager, but the answer never came, not at that time. You probably think that this was the worst thing that a teenager can do only to help.

As I said, I did a lot of stupid things as a teenager but these two were the worst and I am still sorry about that, really I am.🙏

You know, my lovely, my Grandpa was a very rich man. I'm sure you're now thinking: "Oh no, he's going to steal some money from his Grandpa!"

No, my lovely, I never even thought about that, but we were hoping that he would help us because he was really rich, but he didn't. Everybody knew how much money he had. He had the first and the biggest baker's shop in our town at that time.

But he didn't help us and I never ever thought about stealing money from him until something happened one day.

I was desperate to somehow to help my Dad, to get him out of this situation.

Without telling him that I was looking for a way to help him, of course.

A few months after my Grandma died (she was a lovely Grandma), my Grandpa got very sick and I think he knew that he would die soon, too.

One day I went into his room without knocking and I saw him giving a lot of money to my cousin. I was so angry and mad because we didn't have money to buy food, my Dad was down and out, and my Grandpa was giving his all money to my cousin and to my uncle?!

Without dividing the money into three equal parts, one part for my Dad, one part for his brother and one part for his sister.

No, everybody received their share except my Dad.

I couldn't let that go just like that. Maybe my Dad could, but I couldn't.

One day the house was empty and I checked every corner in the house, but I didn't find my Grandpa's big money, only a little to buy a new pair of shoes for me. The big money was already in the pockets of my uncle and my aunt. He died a few months after that.

Grandpa, I'm sorry that I stole some money from you a few months before you died, but Grandpa, that was just not fair!! But I forgive you, and I hope you forgive me too. Rest in peace Grandpa. 🙏

My Dad went broke without his stores, without his job, and without his parents. I know that was a very bad time for you Dad, but believe me Dad, I did everything I could to help you, but it didn't work out.

I was so sorry for him.

He was ruined.

He didn't want to leave the house.

Everybody turned their back on him.

13

He was not an evil man.

He didn't deserve that.

I was so sorry for him.

But the show must go on, my lovely, and my parents needed to find a way to point us in the right direction. Like all other parents they didn't want to give up just like that, and they couldn't. In their own way, my parents wanted the best for me, and they thought I needed to go to college, because my sister was at college and now they thought it was my turn, even though I didn't want to study, at least not for a few years until I had figured out what I wanted to study, but they insisted. The only problem was, as always, the money.

Thank God, in the meanwhile my sister had come back from her studies and she had found a job in our hometown, and she helped me a lot financially.

Thank you sister. ♥

And my Dad was also close to finding a job, only unfortunately the job was rather far away from our small town, in fact it was very far away, in Russia.

It's true that we didn't have the best relationship, but deep inside I didn't want him to go so far away from us, but it was the only way in which he could provide me with the opportunity to study.

Now the choice was left to me to find a college.

Up to me?

I was like a wild beast in my high school years, and now I was supposed to be grown up enough to find a proper college?

First of all, I didn't want to study, and secondly I had a very hard time at high school, and thirdly I missed the first application period. In the second application period they had no more places available in the "normal" colleges. I am not saying that my college wasn't normal. ☺ For me it was the only choice at that time.

From today's point of view, the right one. And which subjects were available?

There were a few places free in philosophy. I thought, "I hate philosophy."

I used to yell at the philosophy teacher at high school like crazy. I couldn't study that.

Then I thought: you can choose between two evils, Jane.

You can stay here with your Mom and your sister, of course, in 35m2 of living space.

Or you can go and study what you don't want to study.

It's up to you, Jane.

I thought, "Why not."

Philosophy is not so bad 😀, by the way,

I didn't want to stay in our small town and in our 35m2 of paradise.

I don't have anything against anybody and I was happy for the people who were content to live in our small town, but I wasn't.

I had to find my way.

With his help.

Thank God something has guided me my whole life, and even in some moments when I thought that I didn't know what I was doing, He knew.

And I was there.

With the help of my Dad, my sister and my Mom, I had the opportunity to study in a big town.

And I thought, "I won't disappoint you guys,

you're giving your best and I'm going to make you proud one day."

My first year as a student was the best year. We had a huge apartment in the city center, and that was a great experience for me. I was living with my good friend who is now a very successful man. I am so happy for him.

In this first year I had the opportunity to meet a lot of new people and that was really a nice year for me. But after the first year I saw that my parents were struggling with money, and with the excuse that I wanted to see the other side of college life I decide to leave the apartment and go to a hall of residence.

But I was not only thinking about changing where I lived, I was ready to leave the country.

After only one year of studying, I saw that I didn't have a future at that college.

My parents always taught me that I should finish college, find a job and be comfortably off for the rest of my life.

With a salary of 250 euros per month after finishing college I didn't think that you could be a comfortably off just like that?

Then I had the idea to go to the USA.

I had a friend there and I called him and told him that I wanted to come to the USA.

He told me what I was supposed to do and I did it.

I applied to an agency and they found me a job in Ohio where my friend was. And then the only thing left was to get the visa.

I thought that was it.

In my mind I was already there.

I was earning money and making something out of my life.

But?

I didn't get the visa.

I was so disappointed when I came out of the US Embassy that for a moment I thought I would jump under a car and everything would be ok.

That was the only way the next Columbo could be stopped.☺

Let's say I wanted more from my life.

So, I had to go back to my studies.

I thought, "Super, another wasted year of waiting for me."

Another start from zero in a new environment.

Almost every year I moved to a different hall of residence. From one point of view, that was a nice experience because I met a lot of people and I had friends in almost every city, but from another point of view it was not so funny sometimes, with four people in 15m2, that was really not pleasant.

Then the second year was almost over. And I didn't want to stay in my hometown during the summer so I applied to work in Greece.

That was a nice experience.

A really nice experience, if I only forget the fact that my roommate was a professional thief and stole everything from mobile phones to bags and laptops, and without telling anyone he hid everything he stole in the back yard where we drank coffee every morning. One day ten cops came with three dogs and they turned over the whole back yard and the apartments where we were sleeping, and they found everything. If I could somehow forget that, this working and travelling experience could have been one of the best in my life. When I came back from Greece I began the third year of my course, again in a new environment and in another hall of residence.

I had almost enough of these new environments. I thought that when I had finished my third and fourth year I would find a job, as a waiter of course, and then I would find an apartment, because I could only afford an apartment with a job, and by working I could help my parents a little by releasing them slightly from the obligation to pay for everything.

At that time my sister was helping me a lot and I am grateful for that. I was also always there for her when she needed me. That's exactly the point, isn't it? Family members who help each other when they can and as much as they can without looking who has given more, or who gives less, or who has more or who has less. Or is that just my way of thinking?

In any case, we had a wonderful relationship with each other.

As I said, I finished my fourth year and I found a job as a waiter (I was and I still am a man of my word) ☺ and I worked as waiter for a year and a half, and in the meanwhile I finished my college and I worked for a year as an ethics teacher, then I worked in a 24-hour kiosk for almost two years.

That was the way I paid my rent and bought my food. I didn't have the money for other things.

My family helped me as much as they could.

I was and am grateful for that, but I am their child, and isn't that the way parents give unconditional love?

To give with love what they have, expecting nothing in return?

Or is that just my way of thinking?

Anyway, in the meanwhile I didn't want to pay rent any more, and I wanted to buy a small apartment of 35m2 or more. As I said, I wanted more from my life and that was my biggest dream, to have my own piece of space.

I was no longer the bad kid from the high school; I had finished university and I was doing any work I could find at that time.

I couldn't afford to buy this small apartment alone, I needed help from my family.

My relationship with my Mom was even better, and I thought I would speak to her.

First, I found a small place where we could build a small house.

But she said to my Dad that the neighborhood was not so good, and they didn't support me. The second time I found a 40m2 apartment and I only needed my Mom to sign to get the ok from the bank, but she didn't.

Then I finally realized.

I realized something very important.

I realized what I hadn't been able to see twice before: the first time as a child with the Karate and music lessons and the second time as a 19-year-old guy.

At the age of 26 I finally realized that if I wanted to achieve something in my life, I had to do it by myself, and that was the biggest lesson that I learned from my parents.

Thank you for that Mom and Dad.

I really mean that.

Thank you from my ♡

Then came the time to take control of my own life.

I found a guy who had a construction company in France. I was ready to go, to leave everything behind me, even without saying goodbye.

And I did it.

I was disappointed once again, but this time even more so.

Nothing that I did was ever enough.

I finished my college and it was not enough.

I worked in every job that I could find from cleaning to being a teacher only to earn a little money, and that was not enough.

I wanted to show that I was responsible enough, and, with a little help from my parents, to finally buy a 35m2 living space where I could begin my own life, but it was not enough.

Yes, I learned a very helpful lesson for a lifetime, but I was disappointed at that moment and I was ready to go. Nobody believed me that I was ready to go.

In a few months I was finally ready to fly to France.

My Mom was so mad at me.

She was so angry with me that the night before I flew to Paris we had argument and she hit me.

At the age of 27 she hit me.

Did she hit me only because I wanted to earn some money for a better life?

Did she hit me only because I wanted to find my way?

Dear Mom, I was so unhappy and I was struggling every month to get by, but you couldn't see that, you were only afraid of being left alone, that's why you hit me!

With all respect, my dear Mom, I am not you husband who will always be with you, I will be always there *for* you, when you need me, but not always be *with* you. Another man is responsible for that, not me, my dear Mom.

I am your son, dear Mom, you as a Mom are supposed to be there for me, under all circumstances.

A little advice to all parents.

I am sharing pieces of advice like chocolates here.☺

If, as a parent, you only want to be happy and you are there for your kids only because you expect that one day when you get old they will be there for you, you are missing the point of being a parent, my lovely parents. Your children's happiness is also supposed to be your happiness.

When the child is happy with his or her choice, you as a parent should also be happy.

Especially when the wishes of your child are very 'normal'.

To make something of their life.

To have their own family someday.

To buy an apartment.

To find their own happiness, even in another country.

Especially when your child has followed *your* dreams to finish college even if they didn't want to study, and to find a job and be comfortably off for the rest of their life.

Now it was time for me to follow my dreams and follow my heart.

I was in Paris for three months and I had a rough time with a really hard job there. I worked as a window installer on construction sites - most of the time I was working outside, without health insurance, and I thank God that I am alive today, not only because of the hard and painful job, but also because my lovely colleagues were a liability. Thanks to them I almost got killed there.

They were used to this way of life and they could only cope with the hard work by drinking alcohol, a lot of alcohol.

They drank and went out almost every day after work, but I didn't want to go out with them because I knew what they were capable of, but on the other hand I didn't want to only work and sleep. So I agreed to go out with them, the first and the last time.

We were in some discotheque in the center of Paris, and everything was ok until they got drunk, and in that state of mind the only thing they knew was to start a fight.

All of a sudden I was alone in the disco and I went out to smoke a cigarette. They were already outside and guess what, my lovely?

They started a fight. In those few moments the police arrived with blue flashing lights.

Everybody started running in every direction. So did I.

I was running, but didn't know where I was running and from whom I was running. From the police for sure, and I was also running from those guys with whom my colleagues had started a fight, even though I hadn't done anything wrong, I had just wanted to smoke a cigarette. I thought at that moment that I had to stop smoking, that cigarettes can kill me, literally.☺

Then a car stopped next to me and I thought, "That's it. I'll get killed now."

I'll get killed even though I hadn't done anything wrong.

But thank God there were guys in the car from our group, who recognized me and they stopped and opened the door and said jump inside. Thank God I am alive today.

God has bigger plans for me.

He saved me one more time.

Thank you ♥

It wasn't the best time of my life in Paris and I had this not so pleasant experience of almost getting killed over nothing, but I wanted to stay there, it was better than in my country. I thought I had a future there, that I would learn the language and find something better, as time went on of course.

And that's why I decided to go back to my home town for only 20 days to get something done and then to come back to Paris.

I left all my clothes there in Paris.

I only took the gifts that I had bought for my family with me.

That was my plan, but God had another plan for me.

I was almost four months in my hometown, waiting for a phone call to come back to Paris, but the phone call never came.

That was the only way the next Napoleon could be stopped. ☺

A lot of people in my closest environment were happy that I wasn't happy, that I didn't have a job again and that I didn't get a phone call. The only the problem was that they thought I didn't notice it.

Poor guys, especially inside, deep inside.

I was and still am sorry for you; you are the same even today, almost 10 years later ☹.

What did I do?

I didn't want to wait anymore.

Then I found a guy in Montenegro, actually my Mom's friend recommended me to this guy and told him that I didn't have a job, and he was supposed to help me.

In a short period of time I was already on a bus with another 25 construction workers on the way to Montenegro and with the strong desire deep inside in to make Montenegro a better place for me to live in. ☺

Another beginning.

From zero.

I hated this taste.

For one week I was in his apartment and he asked about a job for me in the hotel where he worked as waiter, but that didn't work out, and then he said I'd have to look for myself.

But he loved to spend time with me because I had a lot of alcohol with me. Nice homemade alcohol☺.

Where I come from people are very creative, and they renamed the famous slogan "Nokia connecting people" to "Alcohol connecting people," and the slogan reflected this situation: we were so connected, we almost became brothers. ☺

But I didn't give up.

I went from hotel to hotel and thank God I found a job in a nice 4-star hotel, but as I've said a hundred times it was his plan to find me a job there, not my plan of course: at that time, I didn't know that.

I was only following the signs, signs put out by HIM.

I was in Budva for four months and I had a very nice time with very pleasant people there. One week before I returned to my hometown I was walking on the beach and I saw a sign advertising a day trip to Dubrovnik.

I thought, "I've never been to Dubrovnik."

I wanted to visit Dubrovnik.

I had never visited Croatia.

I was always open for new experiences and new places.

I asked a few colleagues, but they didn't want to go because they had already been to Dubrovnik.

I thought, "I'll go alone, I came here alone in the first place, and now I have made so many beautiful friendships, and I have never been to Dubrovnik. I'll go there alone if I need to."

I bought a ticket and in the next moment I was already on the bus, alone, on a day trip to Dubrovnik.

We arrived in Dubrovnik, and when I got off the bus a man came up to me and asked me if I was alone on the tour.

I said that I was.

He said, "Ok, I'm also alone.

Would you like to drink a coffee and visit Dubrovnik together?"

I said, "Why not?"

As I said, I was always open for new friendships.

We had a nice time in Dubrovnik, we talked a lot, about my life and about his also.

He said that he was divorced, and he was suffering a lot because he caught his wife with another man and that's why he was alone on vacation in Budva. I was sorry for him, and told him that I was working as a waiter in a nice 4-star hotel and he suggested that he could go out with me and my friends sometimes to have fun and to find another woman, not to be alone on the beach the whole day long or to go on some day trip alone.

He agreed.

I then met him with all my friends; he was close to finding another woman but said he was not ready for a new relationship.

We exchanged telephone numbers and addresses and he flew back to Vienna. In two weeks I was going to Macedonia and that was the end of my experience of Montenegro.

He only said that he had never been to Macedonia and would like to visit it sometime. I told him he would always be welcome in my home.

I felt welcome in Montenegro, my lovely.

Before I left Budva, everybody was crying. Male, female, and I was crying too, I met such nice people there, it was incredible my lovely, as I said, alcohol connecting people.😀

Then I returned to our capital Skopje, where I worked and studied for almost six years to try it one more time.

Another beginning.

From zero.

I really started to hate that feeling.

I found another dream job as a delivery man.

I delivered car parts to shops and I slept at a friend's place because the girl I had been with for seven years left me on the street when I came back from Montenegro. She didn't want to live with me anymore.

I was trying desperately to repay the overdraft we had accumulated when we lived together, but she turned her back on me.

I was desperate.

I was angry with everyone, and with myself, too.

I couldn't please the people around me; no matter what I did it wasn't good enough!

My intentions were good.

But nobody saw them, they only ever saw the end result.

As I said earlier, there are always two plans, your plan about that what you think is good for you, and God's plan about that what He knows is good for you.

That was God's plan. Oh my God, if I had only known at that particular moment, I could have saved my lungs from the hundreds and hundreds of cigarettes that I smoked. 😂

He was just making space for something better to come into my life. If I had known that then I wouldn't have felt so miserable, empty and sad. Let's go on with the story.

I get fired from my dream delivery job after three months, and once again I was down and out, without a job, without money, and now even without a girlfriend.

I felt just like my Dad ten years ago, with nothing and without a plan.

Thank God He had one for me.

I went back to my hometown.

At that time my Dad was also at home, because he had a two-month break from his job in Russia.

Both of us at the same time in our 35m2 living space.

I was on the floor once again even though I was doing my best to make something from my life, but I hit the floor even harder, landing on my face.

I was depressed and I couldn't sleep at all. I was awake almost every night until 4-5 in the morning. I smoked all night long and asked questions.

Why, God?

Why is all this happening to me?

Why does everything that I begin finish in failure?

Why do I always have to start again from zero after ten years of trying to find a way to make something of my life?

Why???

And I always slept until 11 o'clock because I was awake almost the whole night.

My Dad was so angry at me because I was sleeping until 11 o'clock. He had already forgotten that I was doing my best to get my life on the right track, that I had tried almost everything, but it didn't work out. He was just like my Mom: they are the only ones with problems and they sacrificed their lives for us, and we, we were doing nothing in their eyes.

Especially me, because my sister - after finishing her college - had come back to our small town, where she found a job as a teacher and everything was ok with her, but in their eyes I was the one acting like some Marco Polo travelling around the world and trying to find himself.

Even if it had been the way they thought and said, I wasn't a junkie, I wasn't a drug dealer, I wasn't an alcoholic. I was only trying to find myself. But anyway, my dear parents, I love you and I know now from the point of view of a parent that you did the best that you could.

Thank you for everything.

We tried together (me and my Dad) to find some job for me, but we had different views of the world, of life, of everything.

He was and he is still the old-school type: find a job, a better one, and don't let it go until you die.

I was and I am still the new-school type. there must be some purpose behind our existence.

We didn't find anything interesting for me.

His vacation was almost at an end.

Now he had to fly back to Russia.

One night before he began to pack his bag to fly back to Russia he was so pissed off, he was saying all the time that he didn't want to go back to Russia and that he is too old for that, and my Mom was going around like crazy and she was crying all the time.

And what do you think I felt in that moment?

I felt guilt.

I was the young guy who was sleeping until 11 o'clock and he was the old one who needed to go to work. I felt guilty.

For the hundredth time I felt guilt. Over and over again.

Even though it wasn't my fault that he lost his stores and that job in Russia was the first better one that he had found, I felt guilt over and over again.

I went out of the house and I cried and cried and begged God to show me the way. I couldn't take any more of this pressure. For an hour I sat outside and I cried like a small 27-year-old child.

And then what happened my lovely?

A few days later the guy I had met in Dubrovnik called me.

He wanted to visit Macedonia.

Even though I was in total chaos I organized everything for him to come and visit Macedonia. He was in Macedonia for three days and he was thrilled by our hospitality and he said I could call him for help any time.

I thought, "No thanks my friend."

I didn't want to go to another country again.

I had tried America; it didn't work out.

I had tried Greece; it didn't work out.

I had tried France; it didn't work out.

I had tried Montenegro; it didn't work out.

I couldn't try any more.

But sometimes, just by following the signs put out by HIM and by following your heart, my lovely, everything will be just fine.

As time went by I became more and more depressed and I couldn't sit and wait and complain about everything anymore, and I picked up the phone and I called that guy I met in Montenegro and I asked him if I could come to visit him in Vienna.

To try for the last time.

He said, "Of course my door is always open for you."

My sister bought me a ticket, and my Mom gave me 300 euros, and I expected to come back in one and a half months.

I had 300 euros for one and a half months, and I thought, "What a luxurious trip that will be." ☺

As I've said a hundred times, thank you for everything my dear family from my ♥.

My ticket to come back in one and a half months was already reserved.

I thought I would visit him, and if I could find a job in that short time it would be wonderful, if not I would go back to Macedonia.

Another beginning.

From zero.

I hated this feeling. I really did.

I was already on the way to Vienna with 300 euros in my pocket.

I didn't know what to expect, but what happened to me in those one and half months went beyond even my wildest dreams.

He was waiting for me at the airport and we went to his apartment.

I took a few steps inside and I already felt something wasn't right.

Believe me my lovely, I can smell a bad person from a mile away - he wasn't a bad person, but something was not right.

I could feel that. We went out two times in the first week and we had really good time, but something was not ok.

In this first week I already saw that he hadn't been very honest with me.

I saw we were from different worlds, in every single way.

He had told me that he was married and now he was divorced, but the truth was different.

He had never married.

I found a lot of pictures in his apartment of a guy who looked exactly like me.

"Oh my God," I thought.

He is gay.

Why didn't I see that when we first met?

Oh my God, maybe he's in love in me and now I am stuck in his apartment without friends, with 300 euros in my pocket and with no knowledge of the language and the city.

I thought that was the truth!

Definitely.

That he saw his ex in me because we looked similar.

He fell in love in me and now I am in his apartment and I don't have the money to go back just like that, I have to stay one and a half months because my return ticket is already reserved and I have to stay here with this guy who said that he had been married, but the truth was that he was looking at me in a different way.

I couldn't believe it.

This is not happening to me.

Noooo!

Why me, God!

One day he was working and I called him and I told him that I was waiting for him in his apartment and we needed to talk about something serious.

I told him that I knew the truth but I needed to hear it from him.

He said, "Yes Jane, I am sorry, I am gay. I am sorry that I lied you but I couldn't tell you just like that because I knew you would never even talk to me."

My face turned red.

I yelled and screamed at him. I was so pissed off because he had lied to me.

Don't get me wrong, my lovely, I don't have anything against gay people, I really don't, but he had looked in my eyes and lied to me and had said he wanted to visit my country, and all the time he was obviously planning something else in his head.

I was scared because I found myself in another country with a guy who was secretly in love in me and I didn't have any friends there. I didn't know the city and I had only 300 euros in my pocket!

But when the lion is hurt, then it is at its most dangerous. I didn't show him how scared I was.

But what hurt me most, my lovely, is that I had been so sorry for him when he told me in Montenegro that he had caught his wife with another guy and that his heart was broken and he would never recover from what had happened to him. I remember that I almost cried when he said that to me in Montenegro.

That hurts, because I was really sorry for him and he was lying to my face without any problem.

That's why I was so pissed off, not because of the fact that he was gay!

I didn't know what to do.

I couldn't speak to him because he had lied to me, not because he was gay.

I couldn't go back to Macedonia after only one week.

I couldn't stay there.

Oh my God!

Oh my Godddd!

Why!

He apologized a hundred times and he promised me that he would be there for me when I needed him, and if I didn't want to speak with him, he could totally understand that.

He wasn't a bad person.

He was just not brave enough to tell me to my face who he really was.

If he had told me that when we first met we could certainly have become and stayed friends. Why not?!

He can chase boys; I will chase girls and we could be friends.

I really don't have anything against the gay population. I really don't.

But in this way, behind my back, to lie to me.

No way.

No way!

I was devastated again.

I hated this feeling.

I really did.

Every time I planned something good, something bad happened!

One more time from zero.

Why?

Whyyy God?!

Every day before he came home from his job, I went out.

I didn't know where I was going.

I just couldn't look him in the eye because in my eyes he was not a man, he was a coward because he was not brave enough to stand up for what he really was.

I even told him that.

Because I saw he was hiding his sexual orientation not only from me but from 50% of his friends: they didn't know anything either. He actually admitted that to me, he said, "Jane, I'm afraid of how my environment would react if they found out – that's why most of my friends don't actually know." I told him they would react just like I reacted, they would be disappointed in him as a person. They would not be disappointed because he is gay, because that is his life and he can do what he wants with his life, but as a person they would definitely be disappointed, just like I was, because he was one big liar. And as I said, I went out every single day when he came home and I just walked and walked.

I walked up and down the same street in Vienna for a month.

I sat in the same park for a month.

I was smoking and trying to figure things out.

I couldn't go back to my hometown any more.

I couldn't stay here either.

Why is this happening to me!?

I was asking myself what was going on here?

I had finished university.

I wasn't stupid.

I had worked in 20 different jobs.

I wasn't lazy.

What is going on with my life?

On the other hand, I couldn't stay there. We were avoiding each other all the time, even though he felt guilty and he was trying to make up for it, but I was distraught. He had lied to me about something that he certainly shouldn't have lied about.

He even found me a part-time job as a waiter so that I would forgive him.

He bought me cigarettes every day and he left them on the table early in the morning, because he knew I wouldn't be there when he came back from his job.

He saw that I was a decent, normal and honest guy.

He saw that if he had been honest with me from the beginning he could have had a real long-lasting friend.

But it was easier for him to be a coward. To lie.

My lovely, never be afraid to be honest to yourself and to others about who you really are, because we are perfect just the way we are, straight or gay, white or black, big or small, fat or thin, rich or poor. We are all God's children, perfect just the way we are. Time was passing by and I somehow felt sorry for him.

I saw how much he was trying to fix our friendship and I wanted to give him another chance.

One day he wanted to say sorry one more time for that what he had done. He called a girl (a friend of his) and he called me, and he said, "We're going out tonight, Jane, I want you to meet somebody and to come out with us, please don't just stay at home, I'm sorry one more time for lying to you, but please let's go out and have some fun."

He probably thought that maybe I would get along with this girl.

I thought that I should forgive him, even though he had lied to me. He was really trying to make the things work better between us, to be real friends.

I said, "Ok, I'll come out with you tonight."

Even though I was already looking for tickets to go back to Macedonia, I decided to go out with them.

I didn't know at that moment that I had passed the exam.

I had done the most important thing in God's eyes.

I had forgiven another human being for something. Truly, deep in my heart.

When he arrived with her I was already waiting for them in front of the building, and I saw that she was a nice girl, but not my type, and then he introduced her, and, obviously excited, he asked me, "Jane, where do you what to go tonight?"

He was trying to do everything only to be friends again.

She wanted us to go to some disco, but I said, "Please can we go to that restaurant where we were a month ago when I came to Vienna? It was nice there."

He even didn't listen to her.

He said, "Of course Jane, let's go there."

We went inside.

We found a decent table to sit at.

We sat in the restaurant and talked about life.

We had very nice time.

I spent the last of the money I had earned.

I didn't care about anything anymore.

I had come to the end of the line.

Everything that had happened to me in the last few years, and especially in the last few months, was too much, even for me.

And then, as always in life, the most beautiful things happen unexpectedly.

And then the Magic moment happened.

I saw HER!!

I KNEW IT.

That's HER!

The most beautiful woman in the whole world.

She was sitting across from our table with her sister.

That was LOVE at first sight!

I KNEW she was the ONE.

There are very few events in our lives where we just know in that moment: That's IT!

For example, I always knew that God existed.

I didn't know where and how; I just knew it.

Not only because he saved me a few times: I was almost killed in a few fights, fights that I didn't start, I fell asleep at the wheel of a car and some voice woke me up, and a lot of amazing things like that. I just knew that he existed.

And this was one of these moments.

I knew that she was the ONE.

My soulmate.

The other part of me.

The prettier one.

The better one.

In that moment, I thought that was why I had to go through all these things in my life. To lose all my jobs in every country that I went to, my ex-girlfriend turning her back on me, to even almost lose my parents, and to finally come here and meet HER.

The LOVE of my life!

The mother of my children (today we have three of them, thank God, a boy and twins).

This is more proof that God exists, he was only showing me the way and I only needed to be brave enough to follow him.

That was love at first sight.

And how did we meet each other? That is very interesting 😂.In the toilet 😣. A real miracle. 😂

She was going into the toilet, and I was walking behind her.

Inside we met each other.

A magical toilet moment 🙂

She asked me,

"Are you married?"

I said, "No."

"Do you have children?"

I said, "No".

She said, "Then you can write down my number."

I said, "Of course."

Thank God I answered all the questions right. 😄😄

Since that moment I love going to the toilet. 🙂

Every time I go to the toilet there I think, "Yes, I met the love of my life here." 🙂

But really, my lovely, that was it.

She felt the same.

This feeling was so strong and powerful and most importantly, natural.

I told her my story and she saw that I was a "nobody" without a job and with no money, but in her eyes I was somebody, she fell in love with me, as a person and as a man, just the way I was without material things.

She makes me feel beautiful, complete, loved, and for the first time in my life I felt like a man, a real man, because she saw me just like that, as the man of her life. It was a beautiful feeling, my lovely.

Maybe you have also felt like this some time, my lovely?

If not, I very much hope that you will find your soulmate, and in that very moment you will know that she or he is the ONE and you will feel just like I felt, amazing, complete, loved. Until that point I was the Marco Polo who was travelling around trying to find himself, but now I knew that I didn't want go anywhere anymore, I wanted to marry this girl and period!

And when you are in love or happy, then and only then can you see who your real friends are, my lovely.

I knew the moment that I met HER that she would be my wife and after one month of hanging with each other I proposed to HER.

She said yes!! JIPIIIIIIIIIIIIII

And of course I called my Mom and I said to her that I had just asked the girl that I had met if she wanted to marry me and that she had said yes.

She said, "Ok."

She was not very happy with my decision.

I called my sister and my Dad and they were also confused.

And we got married.

Yipiiiiiiiiiiiiiii☺

My family helped me as much as they could, and I am very thankful for that.

Her family also helped us as much as they could.

Thank you too.

Our Godmother helped us a lot. Thank you from my ♥

God bless you and your son.

We found a small apartment and we began our journey.

We didn't have anything in a material sense, but most importantly we had each other.

And that was enough♡

More than enough ♡

A lot of people didn't believe in us; of course they didn't say it out loud, but it was not difficult to see. But most importantly we believed in us.

We were happy and in love, and we are still in love and happy.☺

For my family it was a little difficult to accept this new situation, but as time went by they saw that I was really happy and now they are also happy.

I miss you now just as much you miss me sometimes, but I pray for you every day. And I love you whether you believe it or not.

I know a lot of people thought at the beginning that I was crazy because I was marrying a woman after only knowing her for one month, but, my lovely, if your family and friends do not think that you are crazy, you are not doing the right thing!

Now they also think that I am crazy because I am writing my first book on my night shifts, but I know that I am doing the right thing, just like eight years ago when I met my wife.

I just have this strong feeling inside.

And I am following this feeling and it has never let me down.

Now I had found HER. After 29 years I had finally found HER.

The journey had only just started, my lovely.

Now I had to find HIM.

I had been looking for HIM for a long time.

I had been looking for HIM in church.

Like almost 95% of people I had looked for HIM there.

But he wasn't there.

The teacher only comes when the student is ready.

Obviously I wasn't ready yet.

But I kept searching for HIM.

After a few months of living together I start to work at a cleaning company.

Yes, another beginning from zero in another country, but this time everything was easier, I had HER, and she had ME.

In the meanwhile, I started to learn German in the hope that one day I would find that job where I could finally be comfortably off.

That I should be searching for that had been told to me at least a hundred times, and unconsciously that was what I was looking for.

I thought I was thinking differently, better, on a higher level and not like my parents, but I was thinking in just the same way as my parents, only I didn't know it. And if I had realized it at the time I wouldn't have admitted it to myself.

Every parent's wish is for their child to be better than its parents in every aspect of their lives.

As a parent today this is also my wish.

But if we want to be better we have to think better first, and we must pay attention to our way of thinking and especially to how we behave.

We cannot be a good example for others if we are not satisfied with ourselves. If we are not satisfied with ourselves, we have to change something in ourselves.

Not in others, in ourselves!

In our way of thinking, acting and behaving.

And if we want to change something in ourselves we must realize that sometimes we are not aware of our thoughts, that sometimes we do not behave in the way that we want to behave. That means we have taken on the behavioral model of others without even knowing it, and we have taken on other people's ways of thinking, also without knowing it.

And there is nothing wrong with that: we lived together with our parents for a long period of time and we were in school for long enough to have unconsciously downloaded some other ways of thinking and behaving.

Almost everyone does this. Try to look at your behavior and your way of thinking for a small period of time and you will catch yourself acting and doing things just like your parents or just like someone close to you, like a brother, sister, uncle, etc.

As I said, we downloaded everything unconsciously, but consciously we can change it.

If we want to change something.

If not, then don't ask yourself why you are repeating your parents' mistakes and habits. Because this subconscious thinking is so powerful and stays with us for a long time, even when we become adults. Why, my lovely?

Only because as kids we learned very fast, we didn't know about the past, we didn't know about the future, we were always present, in the moment, and we absorbed everything just like a sponge. 😊

Everything we heard and saw was memorized in our unconscious or subconscious minds.

A lot of what we thought, saw and heard as kids we do, say and think even when we become adults. Unconsciously, of course.

I, for example, have one of my Dad's habits that I unconsciously downloaded.

Not only one 😂, but this was the first time that I recognized that I was doing something that my Dad had done for a long, long, time.

Every time when I caught myself moving my fingers in a circle I knew that it wasn't me; it was my Dad's habit. I only copied it from him because I saw him doing it a hundred times, unconsciously of course.

After that I caught myself thinking and saying a lot of things just like my Mom and Dad.

That began in the same moment as I started to observe myself, or more precisely, to be more conscious about my doing, saying, acting and thinking.

I wanted to change that not because I had something against my parents' way of thinking and behaving, but because it was not MY way of thinking and acting.

And how we can do that?

By being conscious or present enough in precisely that moment!

Only when we are conscious enough, or in other words present enough, to see that this behavior is not our behavior, that this is something that we unconsciously remember from our parents, our friends, from school or wherever, then and only then can we change something.

Do you have the same habits as your parents?

Or your friends?

Have you ever thought about that, my lovely?

If your ambitions are almost the same as the ambitions of your parents, and your parents' behavior and thinking are a role model for you, and you do great things in your life based on this way of thinking and behaving, then you are a lucky guy or girl, my friend.

If the environment in which you grow up is a role model for you and you become a great human being based on that, you are also a lucky person.

But I am speaking here for the majority of people who don't share the same ambitions as their parents or don't have the same way of thinking as their parents, or for those people who have recognized that they think and act just like everybody in their environment only to fit in. Deep inside they have their own opinions and way of thinking, but they are afraid of being judged if they are simply themselves.

What needs to be done?

You have to become the witness of your own way of thinking, acting and behaving if you want to change something.

And then you must have a clear picture of what you want to accept from your parents or from your environment, then accept it. And what you don't want to accept, change it.

You must practice self-awareness and have courage, my lovely, if you want to change yourself.

Maybe you need to change everything, maybe you only need to change some things, or maybe you don't want to change anything and just want to be one of those who always say, "I can't change myself just like that, it's in my genes." For example, "My Dad was an alcoholic, my grandfather too, that's why I'm an alcoholic today."

Maybe you are one of those who wants to be told what to do?

Are you one of them?

I don't think that you are one of them, my lovely.

Everybody wants to have control of their own life, of their own emotions, of their own thinking and behavior.

Nobody wants to be told what he or she is supposed to do.

Nobody wants to be told what is possible, and what is not.

But regarding everything which has been told to us about ourselves, about others, or life in general, the only question is whether we truly believe in it or whether we have our own opinion of ourselves, others or life.

Do you believe the things that people have said about you?

That you are ugly?

That you are stupid?

Or that you are not good enough?

That you'll never succeed in your life?

That you'll never get married?

Do you believe all this?

Or do you have your own opinion about yourself or about your life?

We let ourselves be driven in the wrong direction and then we ask ourselves why we have such low expectations of ourselves.

Because we pick up everything from our environment and accept it as our identity, and we think we are what others say and think we are.

I also thought I am what my close environment told me I am.

No, I am not, and no, you aren't either, my lovely, you are more than that, much more!

Believe me!

But step by step, my lovely.

Let's go back to my story for a bit ☺.

After one year working and learning the language I found a better job. What can be better than cleaning toilets and offices?

A supermarket was better, my lovely.

Can you believe that?

My parents had a supermarket 20 years ago, and for me in the 21st century, having finished university, was a job in a supermarket a better job?

There are people who have walked on the moon, people who have everything within their grasp, others innovating amazing things every day, but was working in a supermarket a better job for me?

That was not my way of thinking, my lovely!

I had unconsciously downloaded that too.

What I am talking about are these low standards and expectations of ourselves, my lovely. Don't get me wrong, my lovely. I don't have anything against supermarket workers, I was one of them, and maybe in 20 years I will work in some supermarket again, who knows, but have you asked yourself, my lovely, why some people are capable of making and creating miraculous things and other people are "happy" with regular jobs. And then they have a mid-life crisis because they understand in their late fifties or sixties that they have wasted their whole life on some shitty jobs and they didn't achieve anything?

Only because of their belief system, my lovely.

Some people believe everything their environment says and has said about them, that they are ugly, stupid, that they will never make anything of their lives and that our human abilities are limited, while other people make a conscious choice to believe in themselves, in miracles and unlimited human potential, rather than in the environment around them.

If you don't believe in yourself, how can you believe in me, my lovely?

If you don't love yourself, how can you love me?

Very simple, isn't it.☺

At that time, I thought I was more than that, that I made conscious choices in my life. But in what I did, I was unknowingly following the orders of my unconscious mind.

Unconsciously I was following my parents' wishes and beliefs.

Unconsciously I believed everything others were saying about me.

Can you remember the passage in this book where my parents said to me, "Finish your college, find a good job and be comfortably off for the rest of your life"?

I was saying almost the same sentence to my wife every single day:

"I'll learn the language very well, and I'll find a job with my degree, I'll go to work in a suit, and there must be a reason why I finished university."

That's the same as what my parents were saying, my lovely, only expressed with different words.

Was it me who said that line?

No, my lovely.

That was my unconscious or subconscious mind.

That was the line that I had heard a hundred times, and I repeated it unconsciously, only with other words.

And that was not the only time that I had heard and taken in something not especially smart from my environment. And this is one of the ways beliefs are created in our minds, my lovely. And the magic place where all our beliefs are collected is in our subconscious mind.

Unfortunately, as kids we remember only the bad things. I heard a lot of them, like:

That I am not good enough.

That someone else might be able to make money that way, but it won't work for me.

That I have to do any work that I can find to survive, rather than doing what I am passionate about.

That as a human, I am limited.

That I am supposed be happy with any job.

That I am supposed to "keep" this job until I die.

That I am supposed to be happy that I can get a loan from the bank.

That I am supposed to be feel ok about the overdraft on my account?

Is that why we were born, my lovely?

To survive, not to live?!

No, my lovely!

I don't accept this idea about not getting above your station.

We have to create our own way of looking at ourselves!

We don't need to believe what our environment says about us, but we also have a small enemy in our heads who collects everything bad which others say about us and multiplies it a hundred times.

Its name is the EGO, my lovely.

We are certainly not the EGO.

No, my lovely.

We are more than that!

We are not here to survive; we are here to live!

We are here to use our full capacity!

We are here to create!

We are here to serve!

To serve to each other.

Believe me, my lovely!

I think now is good time to start to speak about our invisible enemy with a very nice voice and a cute name called the EGO.

Most often it is recognized as this "gentle" negative voice that we have in our heads.

From my own experience I can say that every time when I wanted to change something in my life it was there, it was more than active. :O

And as I started to get closer to HIM (to my higher self), slowly and mostly unnoticed the voice got stronger and stronger.

It knew that I was on the right path and it wanted me to stay close to it. Close to my EGO.

That doesn't mean that this voice came from nowhere. my lovely. It was always there, not so strong and clear, but it was there in my head, especially every time I wanted to make some more significant change in my life it told me that I would fail, that I would never make anything of my life, and it wanted me to stay in my comfort zone where I couldn't achieve anything.

And sometimes it tried to misdirect me.

During my work in the supermarket I would try to find some better job!

And what can be better for that than working in a supermarket?

My EGO mind had a few creative ideas, and my problem was I believed that its ideas and thoughts were my ideas and thoughts.

For example, I thought, "What if a became a supermarket manager?

Then I will feel fulfilled, for sure?"

I tried it but it didn't work out. I was not that kind of guy. And I never will be!

Then I thought I could be a taxi driver.

As a taxi driver, I thought I would have the freedom to work when I wanted to, as much as I wanted, and I would feel fulfilled, for sure?

Then I went to a taxi driver's course and the teacher said, "You as a taxi driver are not obligated to put on a safety belt when you drive, because somebody who is sitting behind you could choke you with the belt. 😳 I thought that was my dream job, but I changed my mind. 😌

I tried other stupid ideas too, but they didn't work out.

I believed it (my EGO mind), and that's why I tried so many stupid things, because I thought this sweet voice in my head called the ego was actually my voice, that I was this voice, that I am the EGO.

And that's why I considered everything which was said to me to be my own.

When I came into contact with a book called *The Fear* by Kosta Petrov, and when I first met it, this sweet voice named the EGO, I knew that I was not the only one who has this voice in the head, everybody does, but only a few are brave enough to speak openly about it.

I thought, "Thank you Kosta for letting me know that I am not crazy." ☺

And if this very successful guy is brave enough to speak about this voice openly and write a book about it, why can't I?

At that time the idea for my own book came, but my EGO was still too strong and I couldn't pull the trigger at that moment, but what I realized was that this voice is actually not my voice, and as Kosta says in his book, I knew that sooner or later I was going to put an end to this friendship.

On a deeper level, I always knew what I wanted to do, but I never admitted it to anybody. I didn't really believe that I was capable of something like that, because my belief system was destructive thanks to everything I had heard from my environment. My belief system was really broken.

But nobody saw that, everybody saw me as a big muscular tattooed guy who didn't have any feelings at all.

The opposite is the truth, but everything is just the way it is supposed to be!

When I met my wife, I knew I could speak to her about everything.

I told her that I wished I could work with a pen and paper.

To write my own book. And not just one, at least six or seven.☺

In modern times called an author or writer.☺

She said, "I believe in you.

I believe you can do that!"

She always supported me.😚

I mean, it took me 29 years and I had to go through half of Europe to find the second part of me and to feel fulfilled in my private life, so why should it be different in my professional life?☺

But I really hope that will happen sooner.

I mean, if I have to wait another 29 years to become a writer I wouldn't have anything against that, I am sure it will be worth every minute of waiting, but I will do my best to ensure that it happens a little earlier.☺

I ALWAYS TRUST THE DIRECTION OF THE UNIVERSE AND KNOW I AM BEING GUIDED!

Let me go back a little to our love story, my lovely.

We were very happy!

We were together 24 hours a day.

We were very happy and we loved each other very much, but we lacked something.

And that was an angel.

Made by love, created by HIM.

We tried from day one to create our own small family, but regarding this subject I always believed that we as humans only have a very small role in creating another life.

I always believed that HE has the final word. The ONE who created us.

Some doctors said something was wrong with us, but I knew that everything was ok with us.

Sometimes we should not believe everything doctors say to us, my lovely.

I didn't.

My wife believed them.

I always kept saying to her that we as humans don't make children only with our physical contact with each other.

I knew that something bigger has the last word in this making children game.☺

I also knew that our first angel was on its way to us.

I kept saying it to my wife.

She had doubts. I didn't.

But in the tough times, we cried together.

I never said to her, "You have doubts, you can cry, but I know deep inside that it is on its way, I won't cry." We cried together like two kids who had just lost their favorite toy.☹

Every time we did a test we cried the whole day long.☹

We wanted to try in-vitro fertilization.

We were open to trying anything only to have our piece of love, but as I said I knew HE has the power to decide when we were going to get our angel.

And we did all the research and we found a private clinic specialized in in-vitro fertilization.

We got frozen four embryos in order to have four attempts.

And then the day came for us to go to the clinic and make our first attempt.

We were very excited.

And scared.

But more excited than scared.

And we had our first attempt.

We went back home. On the way we didn't speak too much to each other.

At home she went in the kitchen to make us coffee and I went in the living room.

I picked up a cross, I kissed it, and I said:

"DEAR GOD, please create a life in my wife's body just like you created your son, our Jesus Christ." I kissed it one more time and put it back.

I didn't tell her what I had done.

And another miraculous moment, my lovely, thanks to God, was now a living room miracle moment, not a toilet miracle moment, like the first time we met, in a toilet. 😂😂😂

She got pregnant, my lovely.

More proof that HE exists.

Don't be afraid to ask and say what you want in your life, my lovely.

Don't be afraid of HIM.

ASK AND YOU SHALL RECEIVE.

And when did she find out that I had done that?

She was 8 months pregnant; we were at home and we were talking about everything in life.

She got emotional and she told me that on the day when we came home from hospital, as she was in the kitchen making us coffee, she felt something in her stomach, something strong, and she knew that she had got pregnant. In that same moment. I started to cry.

You know, my lovely, some bad people out there did everything so that I couldn't have children, my lovely.

As JESUS said, forgive them FATHER, because they do not know what they are doing. 🙏

Only HE knew how much we wanted to have children.

And HE heard me one more time.

Thank you. 🙏 From the bottom of my ♡.

I told her what I did that day as she went into the kitchen, and she also started to cry.

And we cried again, only this time because we were happy.

And knowing that we are not alone makes us cry even more.

HE was with us!!

The most important player is on our side!

Let's say that was one long happy crying evening.☺

Let me go back a little bit to my working life, I mean in the supermarket.☺

In my work things couldn't have been worse at that time.

At that time only I was working, and my wife was at home with our first angel.

It wasn't the best job in the world, but the rent and the bills have to be paid, don't they?

I couldn't quit my job just like that.

But I couldn't work too long there either, because the people I was working with acted and behaved as if they were NASA workers, not supermarket workers.

Another example of how humans can limit themselves.

I also had other issues. Beside all this in my working life. 😂

I was struggling inwardly with my EGO at that time.

On the outside everything seemed to be ok.

On the inside, it was real hell for me.

It was war.

A real war.

I truly believe that everything in our lives happens for a reason, and it certainly wasn't an accident that I came into contact with *The Fear* by Kosta Petrov, and the way I recognized myself in that book was definitely not an accident - it was the first time I was confronted by it, confronted by the fear which was manifesting a voice in my head, in other words called the EGO.

But it is present in the lives of every one of us.

But how can we recognize it?

It shows itself either through a negative voice or through negative thoughts about things that actually never happen to us.

In 99% of cases this negative voice tells you that something bad will happen to you or to your family, or it says bad things about you or about another people, and it waits for a response from you, even if you have not recognized that you are having a monologue in your head about unimportant things that have just happened or about unrealistic things that could happen to you.

In another words, it creates fear!

And this voice which creates fear is only one tiny part of what we call the ego mind.

At first I was a little scared, because I didn't know how to react when it attacked me with a negative thought.

Shall I react with a positive thought?

Shall I say to it, "Go to hell"?

Shall I speak gently with the voice, and then maybe it will let me go?

In any case, I could no longer stand the voice in my head with its announcements such as, "Why did you go to university, Jane?

"It wasn't for this, surely not?"

"Will you end your days here,

in this supermarket?"

"Don't you deserve something better?"

"Do you think you're supposed to be happy here?"

"Can't you achieve anything?"

"Are you weak?"

"You are an idiot who finished university and now you are working in a supermarket."

And more like that.

By the way, everybody has this voice in their heads, but 50% of people are afraid to speak about it, because when you say, even to somebody close to you, that you hear a voice in your head, everybody will say to you that you are out of your mind.

But people cannot understand that it is only when you are "out of your mind" that you can see that this is not your voice, that this is not your reality, that this is something that you collected unconsciously over the years, you collected the whole negativity in the entire world from your environment about yourself, and that is all stuck in your subconscious mind.

On your conscious level, you think you deserve a better life, but unconsciously or subconsciously you are still playing the role of the victim, and that's why you are attracting the same jobs, the same negative people or the same negative experiences that you've already had in your life.

I know, my lovely, it's a little strange when we know that we are at war with our own minds, but we can fix that together☺

Don't worry.

Be strong.

And the other 50% of people think that they actually are these thoughts, and their behavior and beliefs are just based on them.

No, they are not you!

Wake up my Lovely.

Wake up my fellow human☹

And that's why they feel miserable, like I felt. That's why I am writing down my experiences.

To show you that I have been on both sides, and there is a way out, but I was also scared!

I was afraid to speak about it, and at one point I started to believe everything the voice said, but when I saw how many great human beings who achieved great things in their lives were speaking openly about this issue, I wasn't afraid anymore.

It encouraged me to stand up and fight it.

Not literally, my lovely. 😊

Let's go back to my journey, and how I found my true self, or how I found HIM.

My "dream" job in the supermarket was really hell: we got a new boss who thought that he could do anything he wanted; I mean literally everything!

I couldn't and I didn't want to stand that anymore.

I thought I would quit, in the meanwhile my wife would return to her job, and then I would apply to some schools and in that way I would fulfill my calling, my purpose.

And that fitted in with every "downloaded" belief that I had: and that was to be a teacher at a school, a secure job for the rest of my life.

And then two minutes before I died I could say, without being sorry that I had missed something in my life, "What a journey, Jane, well done!" 👏👏

Sounds exciting!

But something unexpected happened, as always in our lives, and especially in my case. I got sick and I was at home for nine days.

And when I came back to my dream job I got fired.

My boss told me that I could work three months more and then I could go.

Can you imagine that my lovely?

After four and half years working there I got fired because I was sick for nine days?

At that time, I was controlled by my EGO mind and I even felt hurt because I got fired.

I felt hurt because I got fired from the job that I hated?

In crazy situations like that, your EGO mind can make you feel bad even for things that you didn't do or deserved.

At that time and today also I was and I AM still very tolerant of other people's opinions.

As always in a some "difficult" situations, you see who are your real friends, and for some "friends" of mine that was good news, but for my closest friends it was bad news, because they knew that I didn't deserve to be kicked out just like that, even though I hated that job. But although I was upset on the surface, deep inside I knew this must be happening for a reason.

One big problem that we face in our society, my lovely, is that the majority of people think that when they do something bad to somebody else, nothing bad will happen to them in return.

I honestly wish them noting but the best but for those people with bad intensions out there I have only one word, KARMA Guys.

I can say only thank you to all people out there who thought that they would hurt me with some evil action, but you know what Guys, you only made me stronger.

Much stronger. 💪

Mentally and physically.

I can send them only love. 🤍

And in this way I came to one of the most important points in my life. My downloaded behavior and thoughts were ready for my downloaded calling.

It was time to learn better German and then to apply to some schools as a teacher.

That was my plan.

There are always two plans.

Your plan for you.

And God's plan for you.

I had been told hundreds of times that I was supposed to run after a secure job.

Even if I thought I was more than that.

More than that conservative old school thinking that I obviously unconsciously downloaded, and I was chasing it even without knowing it. I always thought that to feel fulfilled I had to do something, to become somebody. But HE showed me that I don't.

A few months before I got fired, my ego voice became much stronger.

So powerful that I thought I was going to go crazy.

In the form of pictures, it was sending me everything bad that I had ever seen, heard or read that happened to somebody, and it was projecting this pictures to me and that all this will happen to me and to my family, of course.

To the people I love most.

Don't be afraid to admit that, my lovely.

Not to me.

Not to your family.

But the first step is to admit it to yourself.

That you have this voice that says only bad things about you and about your close family, and that some bad things will happen. They don't happen of course, but its job is to keep you in survival mode all the time, to be afraid all the time, afraid to try something new, afraid to take risks in your life, afraid of life in general.

It also says things about you that are not true.

That you are ugly!

That you are stupid!

That you are not good enough!

That you are afraid!

That you are not capable enough!

At first I was afraid to admit that even to my wife, but I was brave enough to admit it to myself.

I knew that I am a good person, I knew that I am not crazy, I knew that this isn't ME and that's why I was looking for an answer, and HE actually saw how I desperate I was, but at the same time how brave and open I was to ask and look for the answer and finally to accept the answer.

And where did I look for the answers? In church of course, my lovely.

We are all brought up under different religious circumstances, my lovely, and that is ok, but ultimately the time will come when we all have to look deep inside ourselves in order to find the GOD in which we believe.

I have gone to church almost all my life, at least once a week, but in this period of time I was in church a little more, because I knew deep inside that HE exists and HE can help me. I really do!

I knew that he exists because so many magical things have happened to me, and HE saved me so many times that I could not deny that HE exists even if I wanted to.

For example, we went to Italy almost every year.

And one year we were getting ready for our well-deserved vacation.

The night before we were supposed to go I couldn't sleep at all.

I thought we would cancel our vacation, but we couldn't because we had already paid for it.

I thought I would make as many breaks as I could.

And everything would be just fine.

I tried to sleep in the breaks, but I couldn't.

We were almost there, only 50 km to go. I was very tired, but I thought I would make it, we were so close.

All of a sudden my head went down and I fell asleep.

I fell asleep while driving the car!

And my wife and my son were on the back seat.

It is only thanks to HIM that we are alive today.

I heard a woman's voice in my head and I instantly woke up.

All this happened within five seconds.

I realized what could have happened to us.

I pulled the car over to the side of the road.

I started to cry.

He saved us.

One more time.

Thank you ❤ 🙏I really do!!♡

As I said, I was in church almost 2-3 times a week.

I was begging HIM to say something, to do something to show me that I am not crazy. I was very hurt and I cried almost every night, only because I couldn't control my thoughts. What I didn't know at that time was that they were not my thoughts.

The EGO was really trying to drive me crazy.

I was at home, without a job. I was learning the language and waging war with my ego mind.

A war nobody knew about, only I, HE and my ego mind.

One night I was putting our angel to bed and I had this crazy thought attack I couldn't stand and I started to cry.

I thought my son couldn't see me because the light was off, but he said,

"Daddy don't cry, I love you."

That's heart. A lot of it!

I thought, "Enough is enough, my evil friend, I will get you out of here!

I will!!!!

I promised that to myself.

As time went by I got bored at home and I didn't want to learn the language alone any more. Then I thought I would love to be around people, so it would be a good idea to find a German course to learn with other people and not to stay at home the whole time.

Every cell of my body was against going to this course that I found, and that was something that happened to me a lot, especially before some big changes in my life.

My ego mind wanted to keep me in its prison my whole life long, it wanted to control me, to make me really crazy and never to find my true self.

But HE wants me to be happy.

And HE wants you to be happy!

Fulfilled!

To be everything I ever wanted to be.

For you to be everything what you ever wished for!!

Free!

From thoughts!

From fear!

From the future!

From the past!

To be happy and fulfilled, NOW.

And most importantly, to not be afraid of HIM!

HE wanted me to show him that we are ONE.

That you are ONE with HIM.

THAT WE ARE ALL ONE.

Only I was looking for Him in the wrong places.

Maybe you are also looking for Him in the wrong places, my lovely?

Anyway, it's time to look for HIM in the right place, my lovely.

DEEP IN OURSELVES.

As I said, I found a German course and I began it.

The teacher was strange, he talked a lot about himself in the classes, and I said to my wife that I would quit the course because I couldn't hear any more about his life, I was there to learn the language, not to hear what he had already achieved in his life.

But that wasn't me speaking.

That was it.

My fear! My ego!

It knew that if I stayed on the course it would die.

I mean literally!

Thank God I didn't quit.

After a week the teacher said to us that he had to leave and that another teacher would come to teach us, but he said that before he went he wanted to do something for us, he wanted to recommend a book to us which had changed his life, and that after reading this book he had achieved everything which he had already told us about.

This book had changed his life completely.

And now he wanted to help.

And he said, "Boys and girls, this book is

CONVERSATIONS WITH GOD by Neale Donald Walsch."

As I said earlier, my lovely, there are a few moments in our lives where we just KNOW that this is the right thing to do, that something magnificent will happen to us or is already happening to us in that same moment.

I KNEW IT!

I KNEW DEEP INSIDE THAT THIS BOOK WAS GOING TO CHANGE MY LIFE!

I JUST FELT THAT, DEEP INSIDE, MY LOVELY!

I came home and I told my wife what had just happened, and I said to her, "This book is going to change my life."

I hadn't even bought it.

I KNEW IT!

I only showed her the title.

She looked me a little skeptically, to be honest. She probably thought, "I know that you are a philosopher, you read a lot, but how can one book change your life?

You haven't got a job and you are happy about some book?"

But even she saw how my eyes were shining.

How someone there inside me will finally have his chance to show me that we are ONE.

That was HIM.

This light was HIM.

MY POWER, MY STRENGTH, MY GOD.

That was the beginning of its end.

My ego's end.

My false me.

But it wasn't so easy.

It didn't give up so easily.

But I was following HIM and I wasn't afraid at all!

I bought this book and I started to read it.

But the ego wanted to stay with me, and it tried to keep me focused on my downloaded calling and thinking, on finishing my course and playing the role of a teacher.

I was on both sides.

I was changing.

I saw it, my wife saw it too, but it was war, internal war.

Between the ego and my higher self, between the good and bad, between love and hate.

Imagine it like this my lovely: you have a guest who is not invited to your party and because it is too loud and too many people are at the party, you can't remember whether you have invited him or not, but when you realize that you didn't invite him, you would like to get rid of him, but he won't want to go just like that.

That is our Ego.

Edging God Out.

EGO!

We are too busy with our problems, or if we don't have problems we create them by complaining about what happened to us one, two or five months ago and that's why we don't see who is coming to the party in our house (head), and when we recognize the uninvited guest (EGO) and realize that now it is in charge of our house (head), then the war begins, the real war!

Why?

Because it will try to create a lot of scenes only so that it can stay with us longer.

It will say that it loves us.

It will say that it cannot live without us.

It will ask what we are going to be without it.

That is what it says when we do not recognize it as an enemy.

When we realize that it is our enemy it begins to threaten us.

You're going to die!

You are not capable of living.

You are stupid!

You are a loser!

Because it knows that when we get rid of it a new world will open up to us.

The real world. Full of love, and where there is love, I mean pure unconditional love, there is no place for fear, judgement, hatred and separation from each other. And the most important thing is that there is no separation from God.

To continue my story, I finished the course successfully.

Even though I was changing, and I was on the right path to finding HIM, my old unconscious downloaded way of thinking continued: it's aim was to find and secure that comfortable well-paid job that I was unconsciously looking for.

I was only one step away from my destiny, my dream job in which I could finally be happy and fulfilled.

In the meanwhile, I read the first book and I bought the rest of the trilogy by the same author with the title CONVERSATIONS WITH GOD.

I felt different. I couldn't explain it and my wife was also amazed at how fast I was changing, but I still didn't have my ego under control.

I was calm, I was happy just to BE, I was going slowly inside back to my BEING.

From the place where we all come.

And I didn't have a job and I was calm and happy. Just to BE!

Is there something wrong with you?

How can you be happy without a job?

Yes, my ego was also there. But I was at least aware of it as my constant enemy, and I knew that a hell of a lot of work was waiting for me.

A hard time of change was waiting for me, my lovely.

I knew I would need to change my perspective of a lot of things if I wanted to really get rid of it, or at least to learn how to react to it.

I felt different but I still had to learn how to react to it.

I was doing my best and I am still doing so, my lovely, not only for myself but for the people around me too.

I was also learning how to help others to recognize it.

My wife, for example

My first patient was my wife.☺

I saw how she concentrated on the negative things that happened to her, and how she blamed herself for some things that happened in her life, and that is actually its job, the ego's job, to blame you about your current situation, my lovely.

And I helped her a lot.

I still want to help.

That's why I am writing this book.

To help you to recognize it and to be aware of it, my lovely.

But let's go back a little bit so I can tell you how I got rid of it, my lovely. ☺

I was so dedicated to reading this 1,000-page trilogy until the end, and with every page that I read I was closer to it. But my ego was even stronger.

It told me that when I was done with my language exam I would definitely get a job as a teacher and I would be on the safe side.

But it didn't know that I was slowly learning how to react to it.

The first step was to recognize that the ego was speaking, and the second step was how to react to it.

After six months of having conversations with God I was capable of recognizing almost all the time when it, the ego, was attacking me, and when I consciously paid attention to my thoughts I saw that there are almost the same negative thoughts about me and about others.

The bigger problem was how to react.

What it loves to do is to make you believe in these thoughts. By repeating them constantly, believe me you'll start to think they are your thoughts.

And it is waiting for your response, my lovely.

Or in other words, to start to have some type of dialogue in your head about some things that have just happened or about things that are supposed to happen.

Have you had a situation, my lovely, where you were walking along the street and you were not present in that moment and you were thinking about something that just happened or was supposed to happen, and then you see that your mouth is unconsciously moving and you realize you're talking to yourself?

Sounds crazy?

Your EGO is your soul's worst enemy.

Eric Rusty

When somebody sees you from the side, it looks as if you are talking to yourself, but you are actually not talking to yourself, you are only responding to those negative thoughts and you are defending yourself, isn't that true?

That happens to every one of us, but we think it is "normal".

No it's not, my lovely, because its goal is to keep us focused on unimportant negative things, and by repeating them over and over again to make them into important negative things.

I will give you one example.

Ego: So you haven't got a job again?

I: No, but I'll find a better one.

Ego: You won't, you didn't even find this one. You got fired once again.

I: But it wasn't my fault.

Ego: Of course it was your fault.

I: I was only sick for a few days. And now I haven't got a job again.

Ego: You actually deserved that, you were not a good worker and colleague.

I: I was one of the best, I wanted to accomplish something in that job. To stay longer. I was a good colleague; I just didn't want to be used by my colleagues.

I was helping them.

Ego: Not good enough, you're supposed to keep your mouth shut.

I: I couldn't do that, he offended me!

Ego: You deserve that too because you are a nobody.

I: I didn't deserve that, I was always nice to him, I am not nobody.

And then you look at your watch and you have been arguing for half an hour with somebody who actually doesn't exist about why you got kicked out of a job that you actually hated.

And you lost something that you can never get back again, something precious, my lovely, and that is the present moment.

The one and only present moment, my lovely.

Don't you think that's crazy, my lovely?

Isn't it crazy to recognize that some noise in your head bothers you all the time, and keeps you concentrated only on the negative things in your life, but you allow it to keep doing that!

That's crazy, my lovely.

That's why our reaction is very important.

But don't worry, my lovely.

Everything is practice in our lives.

By the way, our brain is only a muscle, just like every other muscle in our body.

Ok, yes, you're right, it's a slightly more complex muscle, but it's still a muscle which can be trained, and it is here to serve us, we are not here to serve it, my lovely.

If our brain – with our help – doesn't make a clear distinction between the working mind and the ego, it will be overwhelmed by its negative thoughts, and with time we will think that these are our own thoughts. And if you think that your reality is a result of your thoughts, and I certainly do, then we have to do something to change our thoughts, and by changing our thoughts we can change our reality, my lovely.

Don't worry, my lovely, we're going to turn it (EGO) from the most important part of our lives – something which has control of us – to an unimportant part in our lives which we control.

First step: recognize that there is a voice inside you, and it isn't your voice.

Now I am coming to the part where I had passed this exam and had applied to more than 40 schools and was waiting for an answer.

The ego, which at that time played a big role in my life, was saying to me, "Now we are only one step away from your safe zone, from your fulfilment, where you're going to be safe and secure for the rest of your life.

And this spark inside me, this light which was waiting for its moment, was laughing at it and was waiting to bloom in manifestation.

In the few months while I was preparing for that exam, I finished the trilogy, I finished my CONVERSATIONS WITH GOD, and something magnificent happened on the day when I finished and I closed the book. More about that a little later, my lovely.

You wouldn't believe it.

Now I want to speak a little bit about those 7-8 months sitting at home with my first angel, reading the trilogy and preparing for this exam.

My lovely, if you had known me before I came into contact with that book and then saw me while I was reading it, you wouldn't have recognized me.

I started to see the light of the day completely differently: the flowers, the trees; somehow I felt that they were part of me, and that I was part of them, and I felt the connection with my fellow humans, the deeper connection. I understood that deep inside we are all One, and most importantly I felt the connection with my source, the Divine, or God, or however you want to call it, and I understood that we are here to give, not to take, to love, not to hate, to appreciate, not to judge, to serve, not to survive, and that we all come from the same place and go back to the same place, a place called love, unconditional love, and that is all we need to give as long as we are here.

I was more peaceful and calmer, though of course I got angry sometimes; I am a human being. But most of the time I was at peace. I was nicer to other people, and I had more understanding for things that I didn't have in the past.

My wife saw my transformation even though she was also skeptical at some point.

But now she is a professional in meditation and self-awareness.☺

I didn't judge other people any more. I didn't want to take part in this judging process any longer.

I no longer spoke about my past, and I stopped being afraid of my future. I started to be more present, and to use this particular moment that I have.

In my mind I wasn't a victim, and I started to understand that I am the creator of my life, simply because

I AM ONE WITH MY CREATOR!

I AM NOT SEPARATE FROM MY CREATOR.

AND I AM NOT SEPARATE FROM MY FELLOW HUMANS.

WE ARE ALL ONE, MY LOVELY.

AND WE ARE ALL ONE WITH OUR CREATOR.

And I knew that something magnificent had happened to me, but I didn't know what it was.

I was confused and excited, but I wasn't afraid at all.

I knew that this was the right thing.

On the day when I finished the trilogy I was alone at home, and I was reading the last page, and as I finished the last sentence I start to cry, very intensely. I had the feeling that I was dying at that moment - actually something really did die in me. I was crying with joy and sadness at the same time.

I, my higher self, GOD, was very happy that we had found each other after 35 years of searching, and that part was crying for joy, and the part that really died in that moment was my EGO. It was crying because it had to leave me after 35 years of friendship. As I was crying I turned and looked up to the sky, and there was proof that the heavens had been listening to and watching me all the time:

there was a heart made of clouds.

I stopped crying and jumped up to get out my phone and take a picture, but the heart was no longer there.

He wanted to tell me, "This was only for you."

For you to know that I am really here where you found me in this moment, in your heart.

Know now that we are ONE, and don't be afraid of anything anymore.

I was speechless.

He was here.

All the time.

Only I was looking for HIM in the wrong places.

He was here in my heart!

Let's be honest, my lovely.

What had been told to me had also been told to you, or at least to most of you.

That the GOD in which you believe - it makes no difference which God - every GOD in which we believe is everywhere else, but not in ourselves.

In the church, in the mosque, in the Bible or the Quran, on the mountain, in the sky. Everywhere else, but nobody told to us to LOOK DEEP INSIDE, in ourselves.

My wife came home with our angel, and when I told her what had just happened, she was also very excited and happy for me.

During my transformation she had also transformed herself greatly, in a positive way of course☺

I was so happy!

I felt HIM in my heart, my lovely.

In the middle of my chest.

DEEP INSIDE in me, my lovely.

And that small talk between us, between me and my Higher Self that I mentioned at the beginning of my book, may have happened now when we found each other or may not have happened at all. As I said, it's all in your imagination and the choice is yours to believe in that or not, my lovely, but what you can do now is to go back for a moment to the beginning and read it one more time, and think about it for a moment. It may make sense to you.♡

A few weeks after this experience I received a big NO from all 40 schools that I had applied to.

I wasn't surprised.

I already knew that this "downloaded calling" to have secure job like a teacher, as supported by my ex-friend the EGO, was not my real calling.

At that time, I didn't know what my real calling was.

But for sure it was not that.

And I know that whatever it is, it will have something to do with helping other people.

Something with sharing the message of ONENESS with our HIGHER SELF.

In the meanwhile, I have to live from something and I have been looking for another job, and we have been working on another child, but as I said earlier, that is not like putting money in a machine so some chocolate will come out when we want it. It doesn't work like that; such things only happen when HE says.

When HE knows that we are ready for it.

The same thing happened with our first angel, and I knew that the same thing would happen with our second child. It will happen, but we have to wait for the right moment to come.

Like the first time we wanted to try in-vitro fertilization.

Altogether we had three egg cells left.

We had frozen two egg cells which were joined together and we also had one separate egg cell.

We thought let's try with this ONE first; if she gets pregnant ok, if not we will separate these two because we were afraid that something bad would happen to my wife and to the babies if we got back two egg cells joined together.

We tried first with the single cell, but she didn't get pregnant.

We were sad, we cried a lot, but everything was ok, we had our angel and we had one more attempt. Now it was only the question of whether we were going to separate them or we were going to put them back together and pray to have twins.

We talked a lot about that, and at first I wanted to separate them because I didn't want something bad to happen to them, to the babies and to my wife.

But I was increasingly aware of my unconscious thoughts produced by my ex-friend the EGO.

Or rather I was becoming stronger, or more precisely, more aware of myself.

I thought, "I am not the same person anymore and I am not supposed to be afraid, not like before, and I found the strongest player DEEP INSIDE me, and now was the time to act fearlessly.

I knew that HE existed, and to find HIM in myself and feel HIM was and is one of the greatest blessings that I have had.

Another blessing that we had received was our first angel and we didn't want him to grow up alone.

But as always, GOD gives us more than we can imagine.

If we trust HIM, ask HIM and if we believe in HIM.

If I had been listening to other people around me telling me what I should do with my life, I wouldn't be here where I am today.

I don't want to say that it was pleasant and that I didn't hear what other people were saying about me, but thank God I always listened to myself, and that myself was obviously HIM.

As HE said in our small talk at the beginning,

BELIEF IN OURSELVES IS BELIEF IN GOD, AND BELIEF IN GOD IS BELIEF IN OURSELVES!

As I said, we had two more frozen egg cells, and we needed to decide whether we were going to separate them or leave them together and try to get twins.

My wife asked me, "What we should we do? I know you were always afraid of the idea of having twins."

I said to her, "You're right. I was afraid, past tense. Now with this knowing and feeling that HE is with us I am not afraid anymore.

Let's put them back together and PRAY that we get two babies."

I said to her that they had been frozen together for almost five years, and I wouldn't separate them now.

I BELIEVED IN HIM MORE THAN EVER.

I FELT HIM.

And guess what my lovely?

My wife got pregnant with twins.

♡♡

Thank you one more time. 🙏

Believe in HIM, trust HIM and miracles will become your reality.

You will be able to manifest everything you would like to have in your life, my lovely.

In the meanwhile, I found a job.

As a security guard. "Another dream job," I thought. "How I am going to make the dream of my own book come true when I can only find jobs like this?

I had to work, I couldn't stay at home and write, especially because we were expecting two more small angels.

I didn't know that this job was also part of HIS plan of making my dream come true, to write my own story about my interesting journey.

My deep hidden wish to write a book was becoming stronger and stronger.

And my real chances were becoming smaller and smaller.

But as HE said at the beginning of my book, you can manifest everything if you truly BELIEVE in it.

For me at that point, the work I was doing was not so important, it was more important to get rid of my downloaded calling and thinking, and to stop unconsciously looking and searching for a secure job which would last a lifetime. And as I said, this job as a security guard was the key to how I could make my dream come true, to become a writer. Are you wondering how, my lovely?

Patience my lovely, a little more patience. 😃

I knew that something beautiful had happened to me, and that's why I didn't stop there. I was looking for more and more information.

I kept searching and reading books with the same topic as the ONE which had opened my eyes.

I was already spiritually awakened thanks to CONVERSATIONS WITH GOD and I can't thank Neale Donald Walsch enough for writing this book, but I was looking for more.

I started to read books by Deepak Chopra, Wayne Dyer, Eckhart Tolle, Sadhguru and Joe Dispenza, and the list goes on and on. And I started to use everything they were saying that could be useful. In other words, I started to believe them, blindly.

I was motivated like never before.

I said to myself that I would do everything they were doing.

I started to do things that I never thought that I would do in my life, ever!

Such as mediation.

I started to meditate.

And affirmations.

I started to use affirmations.

I wrote down some affirmations on a post-it and I put it on the fridge, and I put one that I had written in my pocket, and it goes like this:

Dear God, please inspire me to write a book on how I found you in myself, to help other people to find you in themselves, too. Thank you. This one I put in my pocket.

As I felt that I was ready to do anything only to change my life dramatically, I made another not so common affirmation.

I borrowed an idea from Wayne Dyer to make this affirmation.

In one of his videos he speaks about how, before he writes a book, he first visualizes the book, and secondly, he takes an empty piece of paper and writes the title of the book that he is going to write, and he puts this piece of paper over the cover of an already existing book and places it where he can see his "new" book every single day, hundreds of times.

I did the same thing; I wrote on a piece of paper:

LOOK DEEP INSIDE

JANE DIMITROVSKI

And I put it in a place where I could see my "book" a hundred times a day.

This was all happening in the same year as we got our twins, in the same year as I started to work as a security guard, and in the same year as I started to drastically change my way of thinking, acting and behaving, because I knew DEEP INSIDE that I was doing the right thing.

I worked for eight months in one position, and while I was doing all this, in my free time I was watching hundreds of videos from all these incredible people that I have mentioned, I was reading a lot while everybody else went to bed at home, and I was repeating these affirmations every single day, hundreds of times, but in my job I couldn't do much because I had a lot to do on my day shifts and also on my night shifts.

And guess what happened then, my lovely?

In another area of my workplace a colleague became ill, and when I came to work early in the morning one day my boss said to me that I had to work in that area instead of my sick colleague.

I thought why not, and the strangest thing was that on that day I would have actually had the day off, but I had called in to say I would work an extra day because we needed the money: the twins were on their way and my wife was already seven months pregnant.

And I went there, and it was a quiet area; this position was not so bad, and I asked the colleague with whom I was working that day about the night shifts there.

Did you have to work a lot during the night shifts?

He said it was very quiet during the night shifts, you didn't have very much to do; in one 12-hour shift you had 2-3 hours of real work and the rest of the time you could read books or watch movies, but please do not fall asleep. ☺

I thought this was the right time to change the position where I was working.

With my twins coming very soon it would be better to have a quiet job, because at home it was going to be loud enough, J and if it's really so boring on these night shifts I could start to write my own book.☺

I was going to kill two birds with one stone.☺

Yeeeeeeeeessssssssssss!!!

JIPIIIIIIIIIIIIIII!!

I changed my position and I started to work there, and guess what my lovely, after a few months working there I felt inspired and I started to write my own book, my own journey:

HOW I FOUND MY TRUE SELF DEEP INSIDE IN ME! Now I understand why I found this job, because HE already knew my wishes and I believed in HIM blindly, accepting everything HE offered to me with the strong feeling inside that it was going to take me along the right path.

Now I understand that these affirmations really work only when you put effort into it, my lovely, when you believe HIM and trust HIM that everything which comes to you in every moment of your life is for your own growth, for your own good.

As I said, I wrote an affirmation that I would like to be inspired to write my own book, and I was inspired, my lovely. I started to write on my night shifts, on a job given by HIM, because HE knew that I had to have some regular job to pay my bills, but HE also saw how great my desire to write my own book was, and that's why HE guided me to this job and I trusted HIM and followed his signs.

I wrote an affirmation saying that "I am enough," and I feel more than enough now, my lovely. And the last one was that I wrote that I am a bestseller author, and yes, you are holding the next bestseller in your hands right now.

> *"At the end everything going to be fine. If it isn't fine yet, it is not the end."*
>
> - Unknown

Yes, it's work, my lovely. Believe HIM, believe ME.

Open yourself up for growth, and I hope that my experience can help you to also find your true self,

your true self without the EGO, without the baggage from the past, with more self-love and with a feeling of ONENESS. And with the awareness that together with HIM you can accomplish anything.

Yes, this is the way I found my true self.

Yes, this is the way I found my soulmate.

By following the signs put out by HIM.

I only needed to be brave enough to follow them.

THANKS ONE MORE TIME 🙏

Are you brave too, my lovely?

Or do you want to stay in your comfort zone and be controlled by your EGO?

As Einstein said, "There are two ways to live your life. One is as though nothing is a miracle. The other is as though everything is a miracle." It's up to you, my lovely.

And me?

For me, everything is a miracle and everything is possible, my lovely.

I didn't stop there, I kept on searching and I experienced even more of what I felt in the first moment when I read the ONE book: that we are all ONE.

At a deeper level, DEEP INSIDE IN US, we are ALL CONNECTED with each other.

It makes no difference in which country we were born, in which culture we were raised, or in which circumstances we grew up, we all come from the same place and we will go back to the same place.

The place called LOVE.

PURE unconditional LOVE.

In other words, GOD.

Or DIVINE SPIRIT.

Or POWER.

Or SOUL.

You can name it any way you want.

But you must to feel it.

You can't get wet from the word water; you have to feel this liquid on your skin to have a sense of what water is.

It is the same thing with GOD.

GOD cannot be seen by a mortal eye, GOD is Spirit and can only be felt.

And where we can find HIM?

DEEP INSIDE My Lovely, when you say I AM that is GOD of the Scripture,

when I say I AM that is GOD, or the LORD or JESUS, and that's way we are all ONE and connected with each other and with our CREATOR.

Before you put anything such as; your earthly Name, your shape and form (big or small, pretty or ugly), your financial situation (rich or poor), your physical state (healthy or sick), you must to say, I AM and that is GOD.

So far as I am concerned that is GOD of the Scripture.

We are ALL ONE My Lovely.

And when we want to hurt somebody we actually hurt ourselves.

As Neville Goddart would say,

EveryOne is YOU pushed Out.

Now I also understand the words from the scripture,

I AM with you always, to the very end of the age.
Matthew 28:20

HE never left us.

HE is with us always.

HE IS THE PART OF US THAT IS AND KNOWS.

HE IS OUR OWN I AMNESS.

OUR SENSE OF AWERNESS.

THAT'S GOD.

We are told hundred times in the scripture what HIS Name is my Lovely.

> That's why when GOD said to Moses that he should go and free the people of Israel, and that HE would be with him all the time, Moses asked, "When they ask me What is your name? What shall I tell them?
>
> Exodus 3:13

> GOD said unto Moses; "My Name is I AM.

> I AM THAT I AM, thus shalt thou say unto the children of Israel, I AM hath sent you.
>
> Exodus 3:14

That is GOD's name.

I AM.

Now I understand also the meaning of the words from the scripture,

> I AM THE WAY AND THE TRUTH AND THE LIFE,
>
> John 14:6

We use GOD's name all the time, even without knowing it my Lovely.

Every time when we say I AM weak, I AM not good enough, I AM afraid, I AM not worthy, I AM poor, I AM not capable, I cannot do this, or I cannot do that, we are using GOD's name unconsciously, and then we ask ourselves why we are really poor, weak and unhappy.

What you think and what you say about yourself is what you are going to get back, my lovely.

The sentence in the Bible

"Let the weak say I AM strong," Joel 3:10 makes more sense now, doesn't it?

Even when our senses are saying something bad about ourselves we have to use GOD's name and transform it into something good.

We must consciously take care when using the words, I AM, and know that this I AM could be everything we want it to be, good or bad, my lovely!

But we don't want to be weak, poor or unhappy, do we?

If we really don't want that, and even if our senses are saying that we are all of those things, by consciously repeating this powerful sentence we can change our unconscious thinking and attract more abundance, happiness and joy into our lives, my lovely.

Before JESUS was crucified, he asked the Romans why they wanted to crucify him.

They said that he claimed he was GOD, but that he was only a man.

> He said, "Isn't it written in your Law I have said YOU
> ARE GOD'S?
>
> John 10:34

Yes, my lovely, every single ONE of us is part of GOD, and GOD is part of every single ONE of us. LOOK DEEP INSIDE and ask yourself, WHO AM I?

Are we this body?

Are we this mind?

Are we our thoughts?

Are we our education?

Are we our job?

Are we our bank account?

We are first and foremost DIVINE BEINGS, and then everything else.

Our body changes in every single moment. We were kids once, now we are adults; that means our body has changed. We didn't know how to speak one language, and now we might speak 2-3 languages. That means our mind also changes.

Our thoughts today are not the same as the thoughts that we had as kids.

That means our thoughts change.

Our job and bank account can also change from year to year.

Then WHO ARE WE?

And what is it that NEVER changes?

This POWER, this FORCE, this LIGHT, this LOVE, this I AM where we all come from and where we go back to, and this never changes.

When a man dies he doesn't lose weight, he looks almost the same a few hours after his death, because life just left the body, the body didn't leave life.

His life was not his body.

His life was that which just left his body.

This I AM of Men, this power, this spirit, was that life.

This breath which GOD breathed into Adam, that is the life that I AM talking about.

The inner feeling which is behind every thought.

That is where we must put our attention.

Not on our body, not on our mind, and especially not on our thoughts.

50% of "our" thoughts are other people's opinions: about us, about their life, about our life, and almost all of them are negative.

And they stay in our unconscious mind whether we want it or not.

Don't accept the negative opinions and way of thinking of other people as yours, my lovely.

Because this is one of the many ways we unconsciously allow ourselves to think other people's thoughts, and consider them as OURS.

Please don't allow that!

In order to change the world, we must first to change ourselves, my lovely!

The first step we can take is to change our way of thinking and to know that most of these thoughts aren't our thoughts.

Where they come from is not so important, but it is important to be aware of the fact that they are not ours. In other words, they are churned out by our EGO, our false self.

Second step: try - I say try because I know that it is not so easy - to not react to these negative thoughts when they come, and they will come, but try to not react to them EMOTIONALLY.

At the beginning you will certainly react to them, simply because you have recognized the EGO as your own enemy, and when you try to make a clear distinction between you and it, it will become stronger and stronger, but try not to get emotional about the thoughts that it sends you, because that is what it wants, to create as much negative emotion as possible in your body, and later we will see how important the emotions actually are in our lives.

One of the reactions could be not only to not respond to these negative thoughts, but also not to react emotionally.

Try it, my lovely.

To make this transformation more comfortable for yourself, remind yourself every single day that your HIGHER SELF is not separate from YOU, that these are not *your* thoughts, and try to not get emotional about these thoughts. And by using affirmations, create your own positive thoughts, and repeat THEM to yourself day after day and in every single moment.

WHO ARE YOU REALLY?

YOU ARE ONE WITH GOD.

Now we have found out who we really are, my lovely.

WE ARE ONE WITH GOD, MY LOVELY!

We are not separate from HIM.

From this state of Being everything is possible, my lovely.

With this knowing and this feeling inside you, you will never be the same person any more.

I AM not, and I will never be the same person again.

With this mindset, now I AM the creator of my own life.

You are also the CREATOR of your own life, my lovely.

Believe in yourself!

Believe in Him, my lovely!

It is the same thing.

Believe me, my lovely!

Now it's time for another point of view, time for another perception of ourselves, and with this knowing of WHO WE REALLY ARE, and with the knowing of what we are really capable, BELIEVE ME, we can create MIRACLES, my lovely.

Let's go!

With love,

your JD. 🙏

From Another Point of View

Now, to be able to look at ourselves and at others around us from another point of view, we must, as I said, constantly remember WHO WE REALLY ARE!

If we get caught up in our everyday chaos with our IMAGINED problems, we have to find a way to remind ourselves every single day of WHO WE REALLY ARE.

WE are ONE with GOD

WE ARE ONE WITH OUR SOURCE!

WE ARE NOT SEPARATE!

Remember that and repeat it to yourself every single day, make it your everyday affirmation, my lovely, and be open for new things.

If your old way of thinking brought you here and you don't know where you are in your life at this moment, then you have to be open for new things, my lovely, because if you want something in your life that you never had, you have to do something in your life that you never did before. It's that simple, my lovely!

For a start you can use affirmations, my lovely, and if you are afraid of the reaction of others, don't tell anybody that you are doing it, ok?

Then you need to consciously change your way of thinking by being aware of yourself, by training yourself almost every day to see yourself differently, by thinking differently, and finally even speaking differently, my lovely.

And if you see that your thinking or acting is the same as it used to be in some moments, even if you are doing your best, then remove the one important thing from these thoughts and actions, and that is your ATTENTION, and redirect your ATTENTION to your new thoughts and affirmations, my lovely.

This is a daily job, a process, it is not a one-day miracle, but look at this process as if it were an exercise. If you want to build up your muscles you have to go to the gym and exercise, my lovely, and if you want to improve your skills you have to attend some courses and to learn some new techniques, and it is the same thing with the brain: you have to exercise your brain every single day with constant practice.

Repeat your new positive thoughts and visualize where you see yourself in the near future and make a clear distinction between what you were and what you are now.

Between your old you and the new you, between the old way of thinking and the new way of thinking, my lovely.

See another you in the mirror every single day, my lovely, a new you who is focused on your life, not on other people's lives, focused on your goals, not on other people's problems, focused on making the best version of yourself, not on making a worse version of the others!

You can no longer see yourself with the same eyes, especially knowing that YOU are the FORCE ITSELF, YOU are the POWER ITSELF, YOU are GOD HIMSELF.

Don't forget that. EVER!

The same force that runs through you also runs through your fellow humans.

Knowing that YOU are a part of GOD is not knowing that you are better than others.

On the contrary, it means you know that YOU are ONE with others because the same power runs through all human BEINGS, through all living BEINGS. The same POWER, THE POWER of LOVE.

To look from another point of view is actually to start to be conscious about what you are doing, speaking, and most importantly what you are thinking, because thought is one of the most powerful tools we have. We have to learn to use it properly.

Everything we put into our head can be created. Good or bad, it makes no difference, it's our choice. The most difficult part is to be aware that 80-90% of the thoughts that we have are not ours.

We collect them from our environment, family, school, friends, and we transform them into opinions about ourselves. In this way we create a mirror of ourselves and we see ourselves every single day in and through this mirror. And then we don't like the reflection that we see and we don't like the results that we get? Break this mirror, my lovely, and see yourself through HIS EYES!

Other people's opinions about us cannot never be more important than our own opinion about ourselves. Don't let their opinions about us become our opinion about ourselves. Other people's view of our future is not our view of our future, my lovely. Let's start to look at our thoughts and our thinking processes from another point of view. We are the CREATORS of our future. Not others, my lovely. Don't let other people create your future!

If we can get rid of this compulsive thinking and behavior that leads to others having more influence on us than we do, then we are on the right path, my lovely.

You have the key.

LOOK DEEP INSIDE!

> *"No one can depress you. No one can make you anxious. No one can hurt your feelings No one can make you anything Except for that which you allow. INSIDE."*
>
> - Wayne Dyer

If somebody says to you that you are stupid, or that you are ugly, you can argue with them, but you will lose the battle, my lovely. Not because you don't know how to argue, but because some people ATTRACT attention to themselves by humiliating other people. Just because they feel stupid or ugly doesn't mean that everybody feels the same. Say to yourself, "I am smart. I am beautiful," and don't forget you are using GOD'S name all the time, my lovely. Look at yourself from another point of view. Look at yourself through HIS EYES. In HIS EYES we are ALL the same, we are ALL perfect just the way we ARE, my lovely.

But why is it so important to not waste your energy on unimportant things, my lovely?

I will tell you a story.

One beautiful sunny day a wolf and a donkey were sitting on the grass on a beautiful hill.

The sun was shining, the birds were singing, and everything was perfect.

The donkey said, "Look, wolf, this black grass is so beautiful."

The wolf said, "Are you drunk my friend? The grass is green."

The donkey said, "You are crazy my friend, the grass is not green, it is black."

The wolf says it is green, the donkey says it is black, and they begin to argue.

After an hour they still hadn't found a solution and they decided to go to the king of all the animals, the lion, and the king should decide which color the grass is.

The lion heard the story from both sides and said:

"Donkey you are right, the grass is black, you are free to go, and you, wolf, you must go to prison for six months."

The donkey laughed and went away happy, and the wolf began to cry and asked the lion, "Why my King, why? You know too that the grass is green, so why did you say that the grass is black and that I have to go to prison, and the donkey is free to go?"

The Lion said:

"Wolf, you are at fault only because you ARGUED with a donkey!"

That's why you shouldn't ARGUE with the donkeys around YOU!

You know the truth about yourself, and that is the most important thing. You are perfect just the way you ARE. And don't give up, my lovely. If you can't change your way of seeing things overnight; be patient and be aware that this is a process. Don't think that by doing these things only a few times you are going to be able to move mountains. NO, my lovely. You have to do the 'work' every single day, my lovely, and when you consciously start to change yourself, that is when the real war with ourselves, or rather with our EGO mind, begins.

It doesn't want change; it doesn't want something good to happen to you. Its job is to stop you evolving, and its job is also to blame others for your bad life situation or to blame you for the bad life situation of others. Maybe your life situation is bad at this moment, but don't mistake a current bad situation for your whole life, my lovely. Our life is one big changing experience. I consciously use the word "situation" because believe me, just because something didn't happen yesterday, doesn't mean that it won't happen tomorrow.

Maybe yesterday you were rejected by some big boss in a job interview, but that doesn't mean that you cannot find your dream job tomorrow, my lovely. Here it is all about looking at ourselves from another point of view. Start to look at your empty bank account as your current difficult situation, not as a permanent state of affairs, start to look at your bad relationship with your parents as your current life situation, not as a permanently bad lifetime relationship, my lovely.

Everything is changing so fast around us, and that means our life situation can also change very, very fast of course, but first WE MUST CHANGE OURSELVES, my lovely! And yes, we all have ups and downs, good or bad days, and that makes our lives even more exciting. If we knew better, we wouldn't be in this current life situation, but as humans we are blessed with the ability to learn new things.

And we are learning every single moment, my lovely, either from our own or from other people's mistakes my lovely, but to be honest with each other, most of the time we learn from our own mistakes. It is also very important to understand that we are not at fault, we did the best we could at the time, and we don't need to blame ourselves, and especially not for our current life situation, because blame is one of the emotions that we have learned here on Earth. We were not born with this negative emotion, and that not only refers to blame, but also to fear, shame, anxiety, doubt, anger and jealousy. We were not born with these emotions; we are born as pure unconditional LOVE.

The only problem is that we have forgotten that, and we have unconsciously downloaded everything negative around us, and we also put it to use unconsciously. Now it is time to reset ourselves, my lovely! Now it is time to be honest to ourselves that we need some changes in our way of thinking and in our way of behaving, my lovely, and we need to believe. To BELIEVE that we can change ourselves.

Just believe that if we can change ourselves, we can change our environment. If we can change our environment, we can change our community. If we can change our community we may have impact on our city, and if we can have an impact on our city, we can have an impact on the world. But we as humans, we must first begin to change. Everything begins with us. Or better, WITHIN us. LOOK DEEP INSIDE yourself, my lovely. That is where your POWER is, not in your college degree. Not on your BANK ACCOUNT, not in your JOB.

The POWER to be happy and fulfilled.

The POWER to change yourself.

The POWER to change your life.

The POWER to change other people's lives.

The POWER to look carefully at your thoughts and to know which thought you should let inside and which thought you should just let go. You can use your good friends to help you. With them you can recognize these things more easily. Your good friend, your emotions.

Or as others have said, your INTUITION! When a thought comes, look at your emotion. Follow your INTUITION, and if you feel good about the thought you can live it INSIDE, if you don't feel good just let it go. It's as simple as that. You have the power to choose what you want to manifest, and focus your ATTENTION on what you want to manifest, not on what you don't want to manifest. I AM one of the best examples for that my lovely, that's why I am writing this book to show you how we can attract very nice things and how we attract the things that we don't want to happen in our lives.

The first step is to take responsibility for our every action. Not to blame others.

By action I mean what we think, say and do. And if we don't like our current life situation, we first HAVE TO look for a solution in ourselves, not in others. Secondly, we have to start to be aware of our unconscious or subconscious mind. Our unconscious or subconscious MIND is so strong that we can also attract things we are afraid of. That's why it is very important to think about what we want to happen to us, not what we don't want to happen to us.

Think about what you want to manifest, not what you are afraid of, my lovely.

But, really my lovely, when we think about that from the old point of view, we cannot think about what we don't want to happen to us the whole time and expect something to happen which we actually really want to happen to us. It doesn't make sense. We cannot think the whole time about our 'bad past' and wait for a better future. It doesn't make sense, my lovely! We cannot say, "I won't get this job," and then apply and wait to get it. It makes no sense.

We cannot say that we are not good enough and wait for others to say to us that we ARE good enough. It makes no sense, my lovely. What we think, say and do comes back to us like a boomerang. Let's look at it like this, my lovely. The sentence "I am not good enough" is familiar to you. What does this sentence cause in your body? Vibration, or in other words, emotion, good or bad. In this case 'bad'. That is just a reaction from us, because I don't think that anyone wants to feel bad. To react to a good or bad emotion we must use energy. Now we are at the beginning. We are using our energy to find a solution for a problem that actually does not exist. And what is energy? Energy is a power that has no beginning and has no end, that can take on every form. It is power that flows into every one of us.

And what is GOD, my lovely?

Has anybody seen HIM and does anyone know what he looks like? Of course not. Because GOD is also ENERGY that has no beginning and has no end, power that flows in every one of us and can take any form. That means we use GOD and his power, the ENERGY, to solve problems that actually don't exist, and then we ask ourselves why we make big issues out of some imagined problems? Because where we put our energy, that is what grows, my lovely. That's why! If we want to change that, as I said we have to do things that we never did before. First start to look at your ENERGY from another point of view, my lovely.

Focus your ENERGY on situations that you want to happen to you, on things you want to have and solutions that you want to find. Look at yourself through HIS EYES, through the new mirror you have created, and know that you have a bigger purpose in this world, we all do, and be yourself, without fear and without the need to explain to everyone why you are doing everything you do in your life. Do you know why, my lovely? Because people understand only from their point of perception. That's why you should know that you are perfect just the way you are, and if they don't love you the way you are, they actually don't deserve your love and attention, my lovely! We are GOD'S children, perfect in every single way. Loving YOURSELF is not selfish, is not arrogant, it's the first step to knowing YOURSELF better. To find YOURSELF and to find out WHO YOU REALLY ARE. To be fearful and to blame yourself all the time and waste your precious time in this beautiful heaven called Earth, *that* is selfish and arrogant, because HE didn't create us for that, my lovely.

I have been through all this.

I was scared, my lovely, a lot, and I always had the thought that I AM not worthy or I AM not good enough, and as I said at the beginning of this book, I had doubts, I was looking for my fulfillment everywhere, in my parents' eyes, in my colleagues' eyes, in my friends' eyes. I was waiting for somebody to say to me that I AM a good guy and then I could feel good about myself. Until I found HIM in me and saw that my fulfillment is in me, in my eyes, not in others, especially not in the negative ones around me. And thanks to HIM I started to see myself from another point of view, from a fearless point of view, and you can also do that, my lovely. And from this state of Being you can create your own world full of love, happiness and joy, for you and for your lovely family. Full of success, abundance and prosperity, my lovely!

We are created to have everything. I TRULY DEEPLY BELIEVE IN THAT! Not just a good relationship and an empty bank account. Not just a full bank account and a bad relationship. Not just health without wealth and the ability to live our lives to our full potential. Not just money without health. No, my lovely, we deserve EVERYTHING!

I TRULY BELIEVE IN THAT!

EVERYTHING, my lovely.

We deserve and we are created to have EVERYTHING, and believe it or not it's already out there, we only need to grab it! Not just because we are here in this form only once, and maybe our life energy will take on another form when our mission is done here, but NOW we are here, and NOW we need to use this time which we have for the things what we want to do, the jobs what we want to work in, with the people we LOVE. NOW, my lovely, not tomorrow, tomorrow never comes. When tomorrow comes, it comes as today, as NOW. It never comes as tomorrow. Another story from me, I feel like a Grandpa telling these stories. ☺

I was working in Greece as a waiter 15 years ago and one night we were out with our colleagues in a city where there were only pubs, bars and hospitals. One bar, one pub, one small hospital and two parallel streets 10km long. I didn't understand why there were so many hospitals, but at 3 AM I understood. There were drunk people everywhere around us, and there were more doctors on the streets than tourists. Then I saw was something very interesting for me: in the bar where we wanted to drink some beers, I saw a sign which I, at that time, as 21-year-old, couldn't understand. The sign said:

Tomorrow 10 Beers Free!

I asked the bartender, "My dear friend, if I come tomorrow will I get 10 free beers? Is that real?" He said "Yes, come tomorrow and you will get 10 free beers."

I said, "Cool, I'll be here again, it's not a problem for me, I have the day off tomorrow. I'll come even though I'm working in other city and I came here with my friends because I heard that here there are the best parties, but for ten free beers I'll be here again tomorrow my friend. It's not a problem!" I was always ready for partying and fun😵‍💫at that time. 😵‍💫

We wanted to go somewhere else, but we were already tired, and by the way we really liked that bar and we didn't leave it, and during the night we got to know the bartender better, and before we left the bar he came to me and he said, "Listen son, don't come tomorrow for 10 free beers, you won't get them!"

I said, "What? you told me I can have them if I come, and by the way, there is a sign here too. I'll come tomorrow!" He said, "My son, when you come tomorrow, it won't be tomorrow, it will be today. Tomorrow never comes. Remember that. Everything happens now." Of course, as a 21-year-old who was only interested in having parties, that was science fiction for me. Tomorrow never comes? What is he talking about? Everything happens now?

I didn't say anything to him, because he was very nice to us during the whole night, but I thought, aha, ok my friend, you are a bartender who knows how much alcohol you have in your blood, now, at this moment, and that's why you are talking about crazy things like tomorrow doesn't really exist, but it's ok! It was nice to meet you my friend!!

But now I understand that, my lovely. Now, after 15 years, I finally understand that everything we want to do, do it now, do not wait for tomorrow my, lovely.

Be present, TODAY! NOW!

The familiar past is already behind us; the unknown future is ahead of us.

The only real thing that we have is the NOW. The PRESENT MOMENT!

If you don't like your past, my lovely, leave it where it actually belongs, in the past, and create a NEW future NOW, use your ENERGY NOW and be in the MOMENT, because even if you create your finished future, and all your dreams come true, you will not be there to enjoy it, you will be in another past or future moment.

If you want to think differently, begin NOW.

If you want to behave differently, begin NOW.

If you want to stop smoking, begin NOW.

If you want to train, begin NOW.

Accept the present moment, because in everything bad that happens to us, something good is hidden inside.

You lose your job, you find another, better one.

Your boyfriend or girlfriend left you, you find another, better one.

You lose your money; you make more money.

Everything in our universe happens for a reason. But we have to be open for a new way of looking at things and a new way of looking at ourselves.

A problem cannot be solved with the same mind and the same way of thinking that actually created the problem. Keep looking every day for a better version of yourself and be grateful for everything you have, but really grateful from your heart, my lovely. And you will see, with time you will attract more and more good things into your life.

Be happy and grateful for what you already have, don't complain all the time about the things that you don't have. Look for more, but first be grateful for everything you already have, my lovely! I am grateful from the bottom of my heart for everything that happened to me in my life until this point, my lovely. Really, it makes no difference whether it was good or bad, there is a lesson to be learned in every situation of our lives. When

I thought someone had closed a door on me, another door was opened for me with more opportunities inside. But I was honest to myself and I was ready to open my heart, and then HE opened the doors and HE showed me that the power is IN us, INSIDE, DEEP INSIDE us. Behind the fear, there was courage, behind the hate there was love, behind the false me, my ego, there was HIM, behind my overthinking of my past and my future, there was joy about the present moment.

And from this state of Being we can attract and create everything we want in our lives, all the happiness and all the joy we can ever imagine, my lovely.

The joy of life.

The joy of being.

The joy of using our full potential and being creative.

My lovely, if I was able do that, everybody can. It wasn't so easy, because I had been thinking and acting in a limited belief system for over 35 years where I was supposed to be satisfied with little and afraid to ask for more. But it's our human nature to want to achieve more, but firstly and most importantly, we must be grateful for what we already have! Period. As I said, I was and I am grateful for everything I have, but I couldn't even imagine becoming inspired or creative with my old way of thinking and with my old belief system. I thought that could happen only to Neale Donald Walsch, Louise Hay or Wayne Dyer, not to me.

> *"CHANGE THE WAY YOU LOOK AT THINGS, AND*
> *THE THINGS YOU LOOK AT WILL CHANGE."*
> - Wayne Dyer

And I did, I changed the way I was looking at myself and I changed the way I was looking at life, and everything changed, my lovely, I started to look at myself from another point of view. One more time my lovely: if I could pull the trigger you can also do it. Be aware of the present moment, my lovely, of the Now! Sometimes we don't accept the Now, not only because the Now is so bad at that moment, but because we think that the next moment or the next day will be better. And maybe it will be, who knows. But what if it isn't? Are we going to wait for tomorrow to be better without doing anything about it today, now? Let's do that, my lovely. Together we are stronger. You are only one thought away from changing your life, my lovely.

Don't waste your precious time!

I have seen a lot of people in my environment, especially people close to me, who didn't make much of their lives only because they always played the safe card, their whole life. They didn't have the courage to leave their comfort zone, one secure job their whole life long without thinking about what their passion is, or how it would be to work in a job which they love, without asking themselves what is their purpose in this life. And what happens then, my lovely? They get fired or they quit because they can't take the pressure of feeling like robots their whole lives.

Then come the middle age crises when they look back and see what they achieved during their whole lives by working in jobs that they didn't actually love, only to survive?

And they see empty space my lovely, nothing left behind them! And if we can screw up our lives with jobs that we don't love, it's worth trying something we love to do, something we are passionate about, and then if we fail we will have no regrets and excuses that others were at fault, and we shouldn't do this or that, because believe me my lovely, something made or done with love and passion has a greater chance to survive and grow than something done without love and passion. Try it my lovely, you don't have anything to lose. Just as I didn't have anything to lose.

Believe in yourself and go for it.

Have you already forgotten that belief in yourself is belief in GOD? And GOD is nothing else than love, pure unconditional love. When you do something from a place of love and you do it with love, there is no way it cannot work out. When you find your GOD in yourself, my lovely, and that will happen sooner or later, you will see that it is all about serving or helping others. This will give you a great feeling of oneness with GOD.

You will notice that results take second place for you. When you see with your own eyes how beautiful it is to have a positive influence on other people's lives, you will be more interested in doing more and more for somebody else.

And everything you give should be given with love without expecting anything in return, or love or appreciation. It makes no difference. Give with an open heart. Everything around us is love and should be given with love. Give your attention and love to your children and be present with them, not only because of your obligations as a mother or father, and expect nothing in return.

Give your attention and love to your wife or husband or partner and be present with them and expect nothing in return. Focus your attention and love on the project that you are working on, not only to earn more money but to leave something greater behind you and to help others, and expect nothing in return.

Make the effort my lovely, and be the BEST version of YOURSELF.

As I said, if I can do it you can also do it. Every single day I focus my awareness on my thoughts and on my actions with one simple goal, to be a better Dad, better husband, better son, better colleague, but I don't expect to be told that I AM a better person now in order to feel good about myself, and I expect nothing in return.

I am not doing this to please others, because I know that in the eyes of some people, whatever I do I am going to stay the same person as they remembered me 3-4 or 10 years ago. Not because I am really the same person, but because they didn't take a step forward in their personal or professional lives, and it is easier for them to play the role of the victim and to blame others.

I don't play this victim game anymore! I played the role of the victim for a long period of time. In my eyes everybody else was responsible for my failures, everybody except me. Then I woke up one day and realized that I was attracting the same people, the same jobs, and the same problems with my old downloaded way of thinking and behaving and that I alone was to blame for my life situation and I take responsibility for that, but now is time for a NEW me, a BETTER me, a GREATER me. We need to be brave enough to think, even for a moment, that maybe we are at fault for some "problems" in our lives. Then to make a few steps to define the problem.

The first step towards finding a solution for a problem that we have is to be aware of the problem and at the same time to admit it to ourselves. It doesn't hurt, believe me, it hurts more when we live on with our old patterns, we lie to ourselves and we don't want to change ourselves for our own good.

Second step: first try to find the solution in yourself, not in others!

Third step: don't forget who you are, that YOU are a part of HIM, a part of the light that actually created you. Be aware of that every single moment of your life, my lovely!!

I AM not saying you should go around saying to other people, "Hey, wait a minute, do you know who you are talking to? I AM GOD, and please watch how you talk with me!" No, my lovely, everybody will say that you are crazy, but do you remember the statement at the beginning of my book? It goes like this:

IF YOU FAMILY AND FRIENDS DON'T THINK THAT YOU ARE CRAZY, YOU ARE NOT DOING THE RIGHT THING.

That's why you shouldn't be worried about what people are going to say about you. Follow your feeling INSIDE, DEEP INSIDE YOU, and just be aware that you are not separate from your SOURCE, feel HIS presence every single day and ask questions, questions that you want to have answered. And the answers will come, and with that the changes, too! Be patient, my lovely. And don't be afraid to accept another point of view of yourself my lovely, and that is, that we are not human beings who are having spiritual experiences, but we are spiritual beings who are having a human experience. Without going beyond our limitations and creating from another state of Being, we can only follow rules, rules which have been made for people who believe only in their five senses.

Sight, hearing, taste, smell and touch.

For example; if I see GOD, then I will believe in HIM!

My lovely, without using a mirror you can't see your nose either, but it is there! How? By focusing your attention on your face, you can feel your nose.

It's the same thing with GOD: focus your attention DEEP INSIDE YOU, and you'll gonna fell HIM without seeing HIM. And meditate, take 20 minutes of your 960 minutes per day.

The day has 24 hours, we sleep about 8 hours, so 16 hours are left: 16 hours × 60 minutes give you 960 minutes a day only for you, and you cannot take 20 minutes to go INSIDE, to stop your mind for a moment and GO DEEP INSIDE? Of course you can, my lovely! TRY it, I can't say what you can become with meditation, because we are all different human beings and we all have all different goals, but I can tell you what I have lost since I started meditating: I lost my fear of failure, I lost my fear of not being good enough, I lost my fear of my future, I lost my fear of my past, I lost my fear of not being accepted, I lost my fear of taking risks, I lost my fear of my ex-friend my ego, and the list goes on and on, my lovely.

Life is not always about receiving something; sometimes losing something is more valuable than receiving something.

Our own beliefs, behaviors, or our own thinking and acting, are sometimes our worst enemies, and when we get rid of these things and we fix our inner world, the external obstacles become easier to manage. All of the authors who I admire, such as Wayne Dyer, Joe Dispenza, Eckhart Tolle, Neale Donald Walsch, Deepak Chopra, who have achieved amazing things and who have told incredible stories, first had to go first beyond their form, to find their true self, who they really are, and from this state of Being they have created all these wonderful things.

And who are we really?

We are ONE with GOD, we are part of HIM, HE is part of us.

We are not SEPARATE FROM HIM, never were, never will be.

This is your new point of view of yourself from today for the rest of your life, my lovely. Welcome to the beginning of your life, my lovely. Send HIS message through, the message of love, the message of ONENESS. We are here to pass on a message, to be the postman who gets the package and gives it to someone else. Without asking what is actually inside, only knowing that this package is going to make the receiver very happy. And we should expect nothing in return, and only be aware and happy with the thought that we helped somebody, and when we really expect nothing in return, then all the rewards, appreciation and wealth that we always wished for will come.

My lovely, I AM just nobody trying to tell everybody about somebody that can save anybody.

Believe in YOURSELF my lovely, believe in HIM.

Believe me my lovely, since I had this experience two years ago with my CONVERSATIONS WITH GOD, and this enlightenment that I felt, and all the books that I have read until today, I realize that everything comes to us at the right time, when we are ready to accept and understand it. We can't force anything, and if we force something it is not natural.

We must to do everything to make our inner world ONE with our thinking, doing, saying and acting, and if we can make our beliefs, faith and our imagination to be in the same team, we are becoming bulletproof, my lovely. There is no obstacle or problem outside which cannot be solved if we are ONE with our inner world. I was thinking negatively and at the same time I was expecting something positive to happen to me; I was doing everything right, at least I thought I was doing everything right I thought I was acting in the right way, but the problem was, I never actually BELIEVED that something marvelous could happen to me because I didn't have the courage to IMAGINE. I didn't have the courage to look at myself from another point of view, through HIS EYES, my lovely! Once I made this transition everything changed for me.

Everything changed in a positive, natural way.

But I had to learn everything from the beginning, and I was fortunate enough to realize who I really AM, and by starting to look at myself and others from another point of view I was ready to fix my last obstacle, and that was my belief system, and to feel worthy enough to finally receive everything I had ever wished for. And if I could do that, you can also do it, my lovely.

As Einstein said:

IMAGINATION IS EVERYTHING.

IT'S THE PREVIEW TO LIFE'S COMING ATTRACTIONS.

Bob Proctor:

IF YOU CAN SEE IT IN YOUR MIND,

YOU WILL HOLD IT IN YOUR HAND.

Don't you ever think, my lovely, that you are not worthy enough, that you are not capable of making your dreams come true? Well look at me, a man who had an enlightenment experience in his apartment which only his wife knew about was brave enough to write a book about his extraordinary experience in his night shifts on the job than You *are also* capable of making your dreams come true too, LOOK DEEP INSIDE, my lovely. TRUST ME.

Look at YOURSELF from another point of view, use affirmations and your IMAGINATION, my lovely, imagine who you want to be, what you want to achieve, and keep this picture close to you every single day. I am imagining you how you are holding my book in your hands and you are crying and smiling at the same time because you have recognized your own fears, your own EGO, your old broken belief system in my story, and after closing this book, I imagine you being ready for a new chapter in your life by saying to yourself;

IF HE COULD DO THAT, SO CAN I!

I CAN ALSO MAKE MY DREAMS COME TRUE!

It's possible, believe me. Can you already see yourself from another point of view, my lovely? From the point of the magical you, who is capable and born for miracles? I see you from this point of view, from this state of being, my lovely, you are SHINING!!

And now get ready for the final round, my lovely, for me the most important one, to get rid of the old belief system that holds us back and keep us stuck, and to create a new belief system and start over again to believe in miracles, because we create them and eventually receive them. Believe me, my lovely, we deserve that.

Let's go!

With love,

your JD 🙏

Believe and Receive

After the first part of my book where we had to make a clear distinction between our EGO mind and its negative thoughts, and after we found out who we really are, in our true pure nature that is ONE WITH OUR SOURCE, we had a second part where in order to change our current reality we also have to make some changes and to start to see ourselves from another point of view, from a more beautiful perspective, to see ourselves as ONE with GOD and not separate from HIM, and now is the time for the final round and the most important thing, and that is to start to BELIEVE and RECEIVE, and really to start to BELIEVE that miracles can happen to us, and to IMAGINE what the end result would look like and have this IMAGE close to you every single day as if had already happened to us, and when the right time comes, to finally RECEIVE IT!

Sounds too crazy and not possible, my lovely?

Yes, it sounds crazy because we have been conditioned our whole life long to see ourselves as separate from our SOURCE, to even be afraid of HIM, and it will take the same time and effort to shift our consciousness, my lovely. Yes, it looks as if it weren't possible because our beliefs are limited based on the circumstances in which we have lived and on the experiences that we have already had, and it will take some effort to change our limited beliefs and our old way of thinking, but it's possible and it's not crazy at all! What I consider to be crazy is not even to try to change something. I am speaking from my own experience, my lovely. Since I realized WHO I really AM and I took all the steps and made the effort to start seeing myself and the world around me from another point of view, I became inspired to write my own book, but that wouldn't have been possible if I hadn't started to change my belief system.

And here is the real power.

In our belief system my lovely.

The subconscious mind and our belief system are the two most important players in our reality. In other words, in a creating a new reality for ourselves! We already learned how our subconscious mind works and understands our language, through repetition, through affirmation and through visualization. Now we have to learn to recreate our belief system in order to CREATE the reality that we want to experience. And my belief system was broken, my lovely. I had to do the hard work and rewrite the story in my head about what is possible for me, my lovely. And what is the easiest way to recreate your belief system? This is the way that helped me and I AM sharing it with you. I started to look at the beliefs that I had as unconscious decisions that I made a long time ago. And in order to change some old beliefs that I had I needed to make a new conscious decision. For example, I had the belief that money is the root of all evil, and obviously I made a unconscious decision as a child that this was true, because my parents argued about money very often, and if I wanted to change this BELIEF I had to make a new conscious decision that money itself was not the cause of their arguments. It was the way my parents *viewed* money!

I had to change that belief and make a new conscious decision that money was the root of all *joy*, and to start to change my perspective of money and begin to see it as positive divine energy with which we experience more life and with which we show appreciation.

Or another example, my lovely: I had the belief about myself that I am not good enough. Of course that was an unconscious process established a long time ago based on some other people's opinions, based on negative school experiences, and the list goes on and on. If I wanted to change this negative BELIEF about myself, I had to make a conscious decision to see myself as good enough, as capable enough, as beautiful just the way I AM, and with constant conscious repetition my subconscious mind started to BELIEVE IN THAT, and that was what I felt, saw and experienced, my lovely.

Our belief system and our subconscious mind are interactively connected with each other.

Our MIND does not differentiate between reality and imagination, and everything we enter into it can be created and drawn to us. However, this can only occur if we are AWARE of the old negative beliefs that we have, and consciously decide to recreate them as positive BELIEFS using the power of our subconscious mind. As I made the new conscious decision that I am of capable of everything I ever wished for, and when I started to use my long-neglected IMAGINATION, helped by knowing who I really AM, and began to observe myself from another point of view, I was inspired to start to write my story, my lovely.

You can rewrite your story too, my lovely. Start today, don't wait for tomorrow, be aware of your false self, your EGO, look at your thoughts as waves that are always coming and going, especially the negative ones. Change your belief system by making new decisions about yourself and imagine yourself in the new role that you what to be and be PATIENT, my lovely.

Be GOD Himself, take any form and role you want to have on this Heaven called Earth.

Here is our heaven and hell, my lovely. With our decisions and choices every single day we are making our lives either heaven or hell. Nobody else, only us. Change some decisions and choices and be what YOU always wanted to BE!

DON'T BE AFRAID.

FEAR is future as imagined by the EGO and only keeps us away from the dream life we are sent here to live. I am not talking about the real fear of jumping into a burning house and burning yourself to death, my lovely! I am talking about the fear, for example, of losing the job that you hate and trying to turn the passion that you have about something you love into a job that you going to adore.

And by the way, has somebody seen this type of fear anywhere, and what does it look like, my lovely? Of course NOT, because it doesn't exist in our reality, it exists only in our minds, especially when we are under the control of the EGO!

DON'T BE AFRAID, my lovely.

AND DO WHAT YOU ALWAYS WANTED TO DO!

"CHOOSE A JOB YOU LOVE AND YOU WILL NEVER HAVE TO WORK ANOTHER DAY IN YOUR LIFE."
                                                    - Confucius

"DO NOT BE AFRAID! THE MOMENT WHEN YOU BECOME FEARLESS, YOUR LIFE BECOMES LIMITLESS."
                                                    - Unknown

Take on every role that you want to play, my lovely, and use your time on Earth to be, do and have everything you ever IMAGINED and WISHED for.

If you want to be an author, sit down, write your story and put your energy, love and positive thoughts and belief in YOURSELF in it.

If you want to be an athlete, train, give your best, add your energy, love and positive thoughts and believe in YOURSELF.

If you want to be the best Dad, the best example for your kids, you don't need to discipline them: they do what you do, not what you tell them to do, that's why you just have to be the best version of YOURSELF and they will copy you.

A little true story about a Dad and his son:

Son and Dad were walking along the street and talking about life. All of a sudden the son steps into a hole in the street and he almost falls down it. The father is angry and says, "My dear son, look where you're walking", and his son responds,

"Dear Dad, look where *you* are walking, I'm just following in YOUR footsteps!"

Make your dreams come true and your children will make their dreams come true. Be the best version of YOURSELF and your children will be the best version of themselves, too.

BELIEVE and CREATE miracles and your children will BELIEVE and CREATE their own miracles.

BELIEVE that you have a purpose here on this planet, a greater purpose, and RECEIVE everything that belongs to you. As I said at the beginning, that is happiness, joy, wealth, and abundance. It is your birthright to be HAPPY and FULFILLED. There are moments in our lives where we think that everything is falling apart around us, but that is only HIM making space for something GREATER to come into our lives.

BELIEVE in that, and DEEP INSIDE be ready to RECEIVE it. You ARE worth it.

I would like to tell one of Steve Harvey's true stories about a beautiful young woman who dated a married man for two long years. They went to the same restaurant every week for two years. This woman had a friend who asked her, "I mean why are you dating this married guy?

You are young and beautiful you can date anybody you want, so why are you dating him, you know he is married! And by the way, God wouldn't send you the right guy?"

And she asked, "What do you mean, HE wouldn't send me the right guy?"

He said, "Because YOU are not ready to RECEIVE it now!"

Then she said, "I believe that GOD doesn't want me to be happy, and that's why he's always sending me these married guys."

He said, "First, *you* don't want yourself to be happy, not GOD; you show that by making a conscious choice to date a guy who is already married, second, you don't actually BELIEVE that that could happen to you, and third and most important, as I said you are not ready to RECEIVE the man of your dreams."

He said, "Let me tell you what my Mom taught me. I was a young guy and I was working very hard because I wanted to buy a new car. I had finally collected enough money to buy a new car.

But every time when I said to my Mom that I wanted to buy a new car she said, your old car is in your back yard my son, you must to make place for new things in your life. One day he cleaned the back yard, sold his old car and brought a new car home and asked his Mom, "Mom why Every time I talked about the new car you said that my old car is in the back yard, tell me Mom, you didn't want me to buy a new car or what was the point?

She said, "Look, my dear son, I just want it to teach you a lesson never to ask GOD for things that you are not ready to RECEIVE them. Never!

And he told that to this beautiful woman; he said "GOD won't send you Mr. Right because you are not ready to RECEIVE him now, you are dating this unsuitable guy."

And she started to cry.

She couldn't date that married guy any more. She stopped seeing him. But she continued to go to the same restaurant.

One day, the waiter asked her, "Why are you alone, madam?

You were always here with that married guy?"

She said, "I stopped dating him."

The waiter said, "THANK GOD!"

She said, how do you mean, "THANK GOD?"

He said, "I looked at you every single week with that married guy and I was asking myself how such a beautiful woman could date that guy?"

Two years later they got married.

Now they have two beautiful children.

Now he is the owner of the restaurant where he worked as a waiter.

That's why, my lovely.

Make a little space for new things in your life, BELIEVE and be ready to RECEIVE IT, because everything we dreamed of is already here, my lovely.

We only need to:

ASK FOR IT

BELIEVE THAT IT IS ON THE WAY

RECEIVE IT

I think that this process of rebuilding our belief system is the most crucial one, because we can put all our effort and time into transforming ourselves into better human beings, but if we don't BELIEVE DEEP in our HEARTS that miracles could happen to us, only based on our past failed experiences or based on our old downloaded belief system, and we think that we are supposed to be realistic, not to DREAM and BELIEVE in something that at the time looked impossible, then miracles really won't happen to us.

In this change process, will and faith are very important players. The will must be very strong and the faith even stronger. Without the willingness to change something and without having the faith that everything will come as it is meant to, we cannot make a single step forward.

The question is: Are we aware of our unconscious flow of negative thoughts and negative beliefs about ourselves?

Do we want to take a risk and to go into the unknown and try to find some solutions?

Or would we rather stay with the pain only because we are afraid of the unknown?

Are we aware that we are actually limiting ourselves?

That we have thoughts in our heads saying that we are not capable, not worthy or not in a position to achieve big things, and we don't even BELIEVE that BIG changes could happen to us?

LOOK DEEP INSIDE MY LOVELY!

For many years we believed that others' beliefs were our beliefs, other opinions were our opinion, and others' thoughts were our thoughts, and it will take some time to clear our heads of this conditioning, my lovely, and that's why willingness and faith are important players here, but first LOOK DEEP INSIDE, MY LOVELY!

And you can find the answer to your questions.

WE ARE LOVE.

WE are already born as PURE unconditional LOVE.

PURE LOVE.

Tabula rasa.

But over the years we have collected some negative BELIEFS and THOUGHTS about ourselves. Now it's time to get rid of them. To remove everything negative which we collected on the way and write a new story, a beautiful one.

A story that we going to be proud of 30 years from now.

We ARE CAPABLE OF MIRACLES, because WE ARE THE MIRACLES!

Every time when I look in the eyes of my beautiful twins I see only that, LOVE, PURE unconditional LOVE. HIM shinning from their eyes without a single trace of fear, hatred or doubt. Only LOVE, PURE unconditional LOVE!

As adults we have all this inside us, but nobody sees through these eyes anymore. The first and most important thing is how we look, then what we are wearing, then what we are driving, then where we work and where we live, and the list goes on and on, and everyone looks at this outside package which we have, but nobody looks INSIDE, first in THEMSELVES and then into the others, and that's why our world looks like this, total chaos, war, hatred, jealousy, separation from each other, and most importantly separation from our SOURCE.

It's TIME TO DO something else, my lovely.

TO OPEN OUR MINDS!

And to be gentle to ourselves and look at ourselves with this feeling of love, compassion and care, and to act through Him, and then take care of the others around us. What's inside comes out my lovely.

I heard an excellent parable from Dr. Wayne Dyer, and that was:

When we squeeze an orange, can apple juice come out? Of course not!

Orange juice will come out.

It is the same thing with us. Look for a moment what happens when somebody puts pressure on us. What shows itself, my lovely?

Anger, doubt, fear, or rather our survival instinct is immediately activated. When attacked we react with a counter-attack. Like animals. Why?

Because that is INSIDE US!

Anger, doubt, fear that is INSIDE US, my lovely!

And we are not born with all these negative emotions we have INSIDE us, we have collected them from our environment, from our school, from our friends, from our family, of course unconsciously, and have multiplied them over time.

If your best friend in school told you every single day how he couldn't pass the mathematics exam because he doubted himself, believe me my lovely, when the next mathematics exam comes you would unconsciously doubt yourself, even if you were very good at mathematics.

Or if you always saw your Dad struggling to pay the bills at the end of the month, and he got angry with himself and everybody else around him because of that, believe me, you will unconsciously have the same fear and anger inside you, it will be only a matter of time and situation until this fear and anger express themselves.

When we know that we are not born with these negative emotions, we know where they come from, the question is what shall we do to not let ourselves be driven by these negative feelings? The first step is to be aware of them, the second to be open and believe that we can change them with our new conscious thinking and acting, and the and third step is to cleanse ourselves. How?

In the book *Zero Limits* by Dr. Joe Vitale I found a very interesting method.

He explains this method using a cleaning mantra from the therapist Dr. Hullen, who used one of the Hawaiian healing methods to help his patients who couldn't make progress in their lives because they kept committing the same crimes. And it worked without him even seeing his patients, only by telling them what they should do.

The mantra is very simple.

It goes like this:

I love you,

I am sorry,

Please forgive me,

Thank you.

His patients needed to recite this mantra to themselves, basically a hundred times a day. They needed to say this mantra to GOD, or to the DIVINE SPIRIT or to the SOUL, whatever you want to call it, to the higher self in themselves, to the GOD in whom they BELIEVED. With this mantra they cleaned out all of the negative feelings inside themselves like fear, doubt, anger, jealousy, and generally all of the negative feelings which were already inside them, without making a difference as to how they got there.

The mantra begins with "I love you", and is to show that we love our creator just like HE loves us, then "I am sorry" expresses our regret that we have consciously or unconsciously let these feelings inside us, and "please forgive me" and "thank you" are self-explanatory, to be thankful for cleansing us of all these negative emotions and feelings.

And it works, my lovely.

Believe me, I used this mantra for a very long time (even though I hadn't committed any crime like Dr. Hullen's patients), and every time

133

when I felt some discomfort in me I repeated the mantra and I felt better, in the very same moment, and I AM grateful for that.

One of the most challenging things is exactly that, being grateful and living in God's Grace even when we are going through rough times. This is the time when lessons must be learned. This is the time when forgiveness and strength must be shown. It is easy, my lovely, to be grateful when your business is successful, when your relationships are great or when your kids are behaving well, but when the rough times come, this is the time when your faith will be put to the test.

The question is whether we can see the big picture, learn the lesson and be responsible enough to admit it when we make some bad decisions that contribute to the position in which we find ourselves. Every time when we are successful in some area in our lives, we say to ourselves, "I made this decision and that's why I was successful," and when we fail we say, "No, that was not my fault, it was his or her decision, he or she was at fault."

We should first try to be honest to ourselves and then it would be much easier to be honest with our fellow humans. We are all in a process of learning in our lives, my lovely.

From our own or from others' mistakes.

Through good or through bad experiences.

Through Satori or Kensho.

I will share with you some wisdom that I learned from the author Michael Beckwith about the idea of Satori and Kensho. He explains how we learn and grow in two ways, through Satori and through Kensho.

Satori is a sudden awakening (something like I had with my CONVERSATIONS WITH GOD) or for example when we have meditated and we suddenly have this feeling of oneness with some higher power, GOD, or the UNIVERSE, or DIVINE POWER, or whatever you want to call it, but these experiences are very rare, they are powerful awakenings but they are really seldom. But, he said, most people grow through Kensho.

Kensho is growth through pain.

Someone leaves you, breaks your heart, and yes, it is painful for you, but you learn more self-love. You lose your job, or your money, and yes, it's painful for you, but you learn new skills, and you find another better job with which you can earn even more money.

You get hospitalized, and yes, it's painful for you, but you learn to take more care of yourself.

These things happen to us only to point us in the right direction, my lovely.

I needed time to realize that, because every time when I lost my job I thought, "Me again, this isn't happening to me? Why me? I didn't deserve that." HE was only making space for better things in my life, and I had to become aware of that, of course with time.

Our problem is that when something bad happens to us, we immediately see ourselves as victims. We don't need to look at ourselves as victims any more, my lovely. Let's look for a moment at our lives as one constant learning process.

Through these two kinds of experiences.

Through Satori and Kensho, my lovely.

And if we only shift our thinking and try to look at everything that has already happened to us as a chance for our personal or spiritual growth, to look at the things that have just happened to us not as problems, but as opportunities to create the person we always wanted to BE DEEP INSIDE.

The BEST version of ourselves.

Be aware that we and only we decide how we feel INSIDE, regardless of the circumstances. Do not let yourself be poisoned by wrongly interpreted circumstances and let the poison get into your DIVINE INSIDE, your PURE unconditional LOVE. One situation can be seen in two totally different ways by two different persons. And that is ok, but don't base your own worthiness on other people's opinions, and try to find something good in all situations. Situations are something that passes by, that doesn't last forever. Again, my lovely, just because something didn't happen in the past doesn't mean that it won't happen in the future!

Believe that something greater is just waiting for you, here, now, around the corner, and be grateful. Please, my lovely, be grateful. Be grateful for everything you have, look forward to achieving more, but first please be grateful for that what you already have in this moment. You have so much that you are not even aware of, look for more, BELIEVE you can achieve more, but always be grateful for what you have. Do you know why, my lovely?

Because everything you have, in this very moment, millions of people in the whole world can only DREAM of. Believe it or not, my lovely.

That is the truth.

We shouldn't feel bad about that: if we can help somebody who needs help that would be nice, if not, their life situation isn't our fault. Just to be aware and grateful for what we have is more than enough. Be aware that we can accomplish anything we IMAGINE. We have so much to offer to the world. The only reason why we were not aware of it until this point is because we didn't have the courage to ASK, we didn't BELIEVE that miracles could happen to us, and if they do happen to us, we are afraid to RECEIVE them because we unconsciously think that we are not worthy of this or that, or that something evil must be hidden behind this nice miracle. Don't be AFRAID, my lovely! We have to stop being afraid, my lovely.

We have to

ASK

BELIEVE

RECEIVE

Because we ARE THE MIRACLES.

You are the MIRACLE, you are HIM!

We are ALL on a journey here, my lovely, to have fun, to achieve everything we want, everything we can imagine, to have this human experience and go back to our BEING. To our source.

We are not human beings who are having a spiritual experience.

We are spiritual beings who are having a human experience, my lovely.

One of the reasons why all these books were written and why I wrote my book is to help people realize that we don't need to go back to understand who we really are, we can understand that while we are alive, here on this magnificent planet.

In other words, we don't need to die to understand that we are ONE WITH GOD.

The secret is to die before you really die.

In this human form we can experience what we have to in order to understand why we are actually here in the first place, and that is to SERVE.

> *"I searched for myself and I only found GOD. I searched for a GOD and I only found myself."*
> - Sufi proverb

That's who you really are my, lovely!

HIM!

As with everything in our lives, if we want to use something we first need to figure out first how this thing actually works, or how to speak its language.

As long as we are aware of the power that we have INSIDE US, we are on the right path to finding the way to work and communicate with this power.

This force, this power, this energy, called God, the universe, divine power or whatever you want to name it, is WITHIN US. Ok now, the first step is already done, we know that is here, IN US, DEEP INSIDE! Now we need to learn how to use it, and how to speak the language that the divine power actually speaks. When researching for my book I found something profound from the well-known author Gregg Braden about the Lost Gospel of Thomas which helped me to understand, learn and finally use the magnificent power we have INSIDE US.

According to Gregg Braden's teaching, the words that I am going to share with you are the actual words of Jesus, spoken when he was teaching the people around HIM how to use this power by combining human emotion and thoughts.

First we have to realize that in almost in every religion and culture, this higher power was recognized thousands of years ago by Christians, Muslims, Buddhists and Hindus. It makes no difference, you can call them whatever you want, but they all agree that something greater than US already exists.

They say that there is a power or energy field, and they also say, which I think is most important, that we can use this power in our human experience only if we know how it works and only if we know how to speak the "language" that it recognizes. This is the gospel that I want to share with you.

In the Gospel of Thomas, in those Greek letters which really existed 300 years after Jesus' time, one of the oldest and most profound secrets about the energy field of this power is hidden.

And that is that the feeling is the KEY!

What does that mean?

That means if you went to a Buddhist and asked them what is the most important thing in praying, he or she would say to you that the feeling is most important, your INNER feeling, to pray as if your prayers had already been answered.

In Egyptian monasteries you will hear the same thing. Feel as if your prayers have already been answered.

And from Christians you will hear exactly the same thing.

And here is verse 106 of the Gospel of Thomas.

Gospel of Thomas, verse 106, translated by Ham Hammadi Liberty:

Verse 106; Jesus said, "When you make the two ONE, you will become the son of man, and when you say mountain move away, it will move away."

He was talking about thought and emotion.

If you can turn these two into ONE, when you say mountain move away, it will move away. In other words, making your thought and your emotion ONE in your heart can move mountains.

He was trying to say that if we can marry these two and make them ONE, and feel it in our hearts, everything which we ever wished for can become our reality.

The Gospel says the same thing again in verse 48.

Verse 48; Jesus said, if two make peace with each other, in this one house they will say to the mountain move away, and it will move away.

He was saying the same thing again only in other words.

If you can make peace between thought and emotion in this house, and this house is you, your head, you are the temple, and you can say mountain move away, and it will move away.

You can create miracles if you bring these two together, my lovely!

In the Christian Bible there is a line which says:

Ask and you shall receive.

Most people ask and ask, but they don't RECEIVE anything.

This is what I meant when I said that we need to learn the language that this energy field, God or divine power understands. It doesn't understand the words that you are saying, it understands only the emotion in your heart as if your prayers had already been answered. Remember what I said at the beginning, THE FEELING IS THE KEY!

AS IF WHAT YOU ARE PRAYING FOR IS ALREADY IN YOUR HANDS!

That's why it is so important to make your thoughts and emotions ONE.

Asking only with words is not enough, ask with your heart and look at your FEELINGS as if what you are praying for is already HERE in your hands.

And then grasp this FEELING and NEVER let it go!

Keep it close to you when you have good and when you have bad days, when everything is ok and when nothing is ok, ASK without a hidden motive, and SURRENDER to the answer.

Be enveloped by what you desire, that your gladness be full.

ASKING without a hidden motive means ASKING without judgment, without your EGO!

This is not the first time that how we should ASK has been told to us, my lovely.

Various writers have told us over and over again to ASK with our hearts and not with our voices, but we didn't hear it.

The 20th century philosopher Neville Goddard said exactly the same thing in his book *The Power of Awareness*.

Then you must make your FUTURE dream a PRESENT fact.

You do this by assuming the feeling of your wish fulfilled.

Then the magic happens, my lovely.

Believe me.

It's time to start to believe in YOURSELF; as we said, that is to believe in HIM, and your life will change.

OPEN YOUR HEART MY LOVELY, BECAUSE IT'S WORK.

This is all about changing our belief system, and that is possible only if we are ready for radical changes. I know it's a radical change in comparison to your current way of thinking, your way of acting and your current perspective of the world, but that's why you are here where you are.

Stuck in your own never-satisfied world created by your own EGO and supported by YOU. Your old belief system brought you here where you are right now, separate from others, always complaining, sick and tired, and worst of all, separate from your source.

It's time for CHANGE.

IT'S TIME FOR RADICAL CHANGES, MY LOVELY!

I lived like you for 35 long years, my lovely, my unconscious negative thinking was always active, always unsatisfied with the present moment, always complaining about the past and anxious about the future, until I decided to make radical changes after I read CONVERSATIONS WITH GOD.

NOW IT'S YOUR TURN, MY LOVELY!

FOR YOUR OWN GOOD!

I know that after reading my book you will also be ready for some radical changes in your life.

I KNOW THAT, DEEP INSIDE!

Now it's time to focus your attention INSIDE my lovely, and don't let the OUTSIDE WORLD control your INNER WORLD. Because everything begins there, INSIDE US.

You are the master of your life, my lovely.

You can control your thoughts.

Your feelings are products of your thought.

Your thoughts create your emotions.

Your reality is a product of your emotions.

Think

Feel

Create

Everything which has been created was at first only a thought.

From a thought a picture is made in your head.

From the picture create a feeling as if you already had it in your hands.

Remember this feeling and hold it as if it were something very important to you.

Surrender and believe.

And your dreams will chase you, not you them, my lovely!

Don't wait for next year to come to change something in your life, don't wait until the coming months to change something in your life, don't even wait for tomorrow to come to change something in your life, because there is only NOW, my lovely.

Now is the moment to change something in your life and surrender to the present moment.

This is the most difficult part. Because we would be rather in our "bad" past or in our uncertain future than in this particular MOMENT: NOW!

We know what already happened to us in our past, and believe me, if we don't get rid of our EGO, our ego mind and our constant thinking about our past are going to recreate our past over and over again, and very soon our past is going to become our future. Again.

That means we unconsciously attract the same things that have already happened to us, only because this feeling is already familiar. And we would rather stay with something familiar to us, even if it is pain and suffering, than really getting rid of it and leaving it where actually belongs, BEHIND US!

Almost the same thing happens with our future. We make plans for our future with the baggage from our past on our shoulders, and even worse, we don't BELIEVE DEEP INSIDE that our plans are really going to happen because we unconsciously think, I know that this or that won't work because of my bad past experiences, but I will try!

If you don't BELIEVE that something is going to work, DON'T EVEN TRY IT!

And we only plan because we as a species want to have everything that happens to us in our lives under control, and we don't want to get surprised by what comes to us. In other words, we want to be familiar with that which may happen to us.

And in this case you are controlling your past and your future.

At least you think you are controlling your past and future.

BUT YOU AREN'T, MY LOVELY!

The only thing you really control is THE PRESENT MOMENT, YOURSELF AND YOUR PERCEPTION OF THE THINGS AROUND YOU.

Change your perception of your past, and don't even think that you are the ONLY one who has to go through all these "bad" things in life. No, you are not, there are people out there with even worst pasts than yours, but they are not complaining all the time! Do you think you can control your future without getting rid of your past first? No you can't, my lovely!

Surrender to the NOW, DON'T BE AFRAID!

And what happens when you surrender to your present moment and become conscious of it? You will be free of your past: without the baggage of your past you will be able to make your future dream a present moment by accepting the feeling that just came to you, and you will stop creating scenarios of how it's going to happen to you. And you will surrender and truly BELIEVE in your heart that it is going to happen, and the universe, God or divine power will take care of the rest.

That's why this BELIEVE AND RECEIVE part is very important.

BELIEVE ME MY LOVELY!

It's time for us to come out from our comfort zone, because in our comfort zone everything is familiar to us, and we think we have control over everything in our lives, but what happens if we stop reflecting on our past and stop controlling our future. What will be left for us?

The present moment, and what do we do with the present moment?

We complain over and over again about our past and worry about the future, and we are stuck in this vicious circle without even knowing it. But why is it so difficult for us to accept the present moment? Why are we so focused on our past and future?

Because if we accept the present moment and be conscious and fully in The NOW, we could, when a situation arises that already happened to us in our past, if this same situation happens again in the Now and we are fully aware, we could react differently, not as emotionally as we did in the past, or with more awareness about the situation. This is a sign of change, but the ego MIND doesn't want that. It wants us to remain stuck in our old BELIEFS that things are just like that and we can't do anything about it. For example: my Dad was an alcoholic and I will become an alcoholic one day, too. My Mom was fat and I can't do anything about my weight. I am also going to be fat.

These are our genes and we can't do anything about that! Yes, you can, my lovely.

You can change not only the way you look, but also your INSIDE world, which is more important, and if you want to make a difference in the world, my lovely, you must first differentiate between who you were and who you want to become. If you want to create miracles you have to BELIEVE in miracles first, my lovely. Everything is in your hands.

Get rid of your EGO, change the perception of yourself by looking at yourself from another point of view and BELIEVE, my lovely! You can do everything to change your life for the better. It's time to get rid of this old BELIEF system created by our EGO and use the BELIEF system given by HIM.

AND THAT IS, YOU HAVE POWER OVER YOUR LIFE. LOOK DEEP INSIDE!

I had the same belief system just like you, my lovely, and thought that I had no control over my life until HE showed me who I really AM.

And that's why I am writing this. So you can figure out who you really are. You are the magician in your own circus, my lovely! Create a journey of which you will be proud in 30 years. I am following my passion thanks to HIM. I am writing my first book and there will be more and more books, my lovely. Because I feel ONE with my source Because I learned to believe in myself after a long period of time. But I am not better then you, we are ALL ONE. You can do also whatever you want to do my Lovely.

Connect with HIM, don't be afraid of HIM. Say what you want to do, don't be shy of HIM. Do you think you are not worthy enough? I know and HE knows you are more than worthy, my lovely! Use 100% of your potential and make a great story of your life. We make heaven or hell out of our lives, my lovely, it only depends on the choices that we make. Don't be afraid and make the best version of yourself, my lovely.

> *"There's no scarcity of opportunity to make a living at what you love. There's only a scarcity of resolve to make it happen."*
> - Wayne Dyer

Life is here and now, my lovely. Not in your past, not in your future. I am speaking from my own experience: I missed so many nice moments in my life only because I was thinking about something that I did or thinking about something that somebody else did to me in the past, or I was so focused on my future, on what I should do to have a better tomorrow, and for most of my life I was not HERE, not in the present moment.

It's time to open our eyes and be aware of every single moment, every single thought, every single emotion that we create or what we have unconsciously downloaded from others, and make better version of ourselves NOW. We are here with our bodies, but not always with our attention. Our body has been given to us, whatever it looks like, it makes no difference, and we need to take good care of it because it is the house of our soul and we have to respect it. However, to think that we are only that, bodies and nothing more, is nonsense, my lovely. I have nothing against keeping our bodies in shape, my lovely.

But we must focus our attention INSIDE our bodies, especially in our hearts.

We think too much about how we look. If somebody says to us that we don't look good, we get worried whether we are we going to be accepted by society and we focus our attention on our appearance and let somebody else have control over our emotions, and we let ourselves be judged by them. DON'T LET THAT HAPPEN, MY LOVELY. For example:

You are trying so hard to look good and you waste two hours preparing yourself for some event to look nice, and then somebody says to you, "You're not looking so good tonight. Are you tired?"

How would you feel then, my lovely?

Terrible of course, because we are forcing positive outcomes, positive reactions, positive opinions from our environment, where we should be demanding that from ourselves rather than from others. And we believe in ourselves only when somebody else does. We let our belief system become warped by our own environment and we hope that somebody else is going to "BELIEVE" in us so we can start to BELIEVE in ourselves again.

Wake up my fellow human!

LOOK DEEP INSIDE

I am not saying that we should walk around in the same clothes for five days, not have a shower and not take care of ourselves my lovely, but to put all our attention on our appearance and on our body without considering that we are maybe more than just bodies is the way of thinking of more than 90% of the population. Invest in your inner world and make your outer world shine.

Ask yourself, "Who am I?"

Find who you really are and shine!

Ask yourself, "What is my purpose?"

Find your purpose and serve!

Ask yourself, "What am I grateful for?"

Find out and be even more grateful!

Realize that your life isn't about you.

"It's about everybody that you come into contact with in your life."

This is one of my favorite lines in CONVERSATIONS WITH GOD. What does it mean? This means if focus your energy on how you can make someone else happy, and how you can improve someone else's life, then and only then can you improve your life. That is what I am doing right now, my lovely.

I AM opening my heart to you and I am writing my true story with DEEP BELIEF INSIDE IN ME that I am going to help you to find yourself and be better version of yourself, my lovely! It took me 36 years to understand that my life isn't about me, that it is about everyone else that I come into contact with. That I am here to SERVE!

Since I started to think how can I help, how I can serve and how I can provide value, my windows started to open. I am not writing to only fulfil my deeply hidden wish and purpose, but also to help others with my story, to help as much as I can. As I said at the beginning of this book, if I can help ten people to be better persons, and to find HIM in themselves, my mission will be accomplished. But I will not stop there, my lovely.

I will give my best to help people, to see happy faces who show gratitude for a few encouraging moments given from the heart. Without a hidden motive. I only want to help, just like somebody else helped me by recommending CONVERSATIONS WITH GOD to me, and I now want to give something back. To help you to redefine your own belief system and to look at yourself from another point of view, from HIS point of view, to see yourself as part of HIM, who is capable of miracles.

A small gift from someone who was so judgmental, so critical towards everybody who didn't think the same way as him, a small gift from someone who thought that the whole world was against him, without recognizing that he was against the whole world, and against himself of course. A small gift from someone who thought that he can go it alone in his life, without being able to see that we are all ONE, and that it is impossible to do something BIG alone. A small gift from someone who was sometimes too honest to others, and who sometimes hurt others' feelings without being aware of it. A small gift from someone who is aware of his mistakes and, without EGO, now has the courage to say he is sorry.

I am sorry for my conscious and unconscious mistakes.

I am sorry for the bad things I said.

I am sorry for letting some people down.

I know what it is like when you are often misunderstood.

When you have good intentions but you let yourself be controlled by your EGO and then something always goes wrong. Apologizing does not always mean that you are wrong and the other person is right, my lovely. It just means that you are valuing your relationships more than your EGO. One of the signs that you are on the right path to getting rid of the EGO is to say that you are sorry even if you know you did nothing wrong. I experienced that myself. As I did with everything I am writing here, my lovely.

My problem was, I unconsciously let myself be driven by my EGO and I always reacted emotionally, and sometimes I said things that I didn't mean, until I realized that I can defend my position without involving my emotion, until I realized that am not what other people think about me, that I don't need to fulfil the expectations of others, and I am definitely not this EGO construction in my head, made by others and of course by the EGO. I AM NOT! It took a while until I realized that. But it's ok. It's never too late!

I AM working on a better version of myself every single day. It's certainly not easy, but the people who spend most of the time with me can see it. If some other people are not able to see it, it's only because they are still under the control of their EGO MIND, and its job is to judge, to blame others, to look for mistakes in others, not in themselves. I am not longer under the control of the EGO. I had to go through this difficult transformation process, but I am finally getting there.

I don't have the same BELIEF system any more, and I also had to go through all of this learning and changing process alone, but now I am writing about my experience only because I don't want you to have to go through the same process that I had to go through.

YOU ARE NOT ALONE! I AM HERE WITH YOU. HE IS ALSO HERE. LOOK DEEP INSIDE, MY LOVELY!

I want you to recognize the EGO earlier than I did, to discover your BELIEF system earlier than I did, and to make to the best version of yourself earlier than I did. That's the truth, my lovely. Otherwise we going to continue to attract what we don't want to happen to us in our lives. That which we are afraid of.

If we don't shift our consciousness, that is going to happen my lovely, because 70% of our day we think the same negative thoughts, and according to research I did, I found out that we have between 60,000 and 70,000 thoughts per day. Can you imagine that, my lovely?

That is between 42,000 and 49,000 negative thoughts per day, and then we expect something good to happen to us? That goes against any logical thinking, my lovely. What is INSIDE is reflected OUTSIDE! Try it for a day, my lovely, just for a day try to get out of your own head and look at your thoughts, be conscious of them for one day only, and you will see the same negative thoughts about yourself and others, about something bad that happened to you, or fear that something bad is going to happen to you. Try it my lovely and you will see. Can you imagine if you just change these negative thoughts into positive ones, or at least if you don't react to them and don't make movies in your head, can you imagine how much free space you are going to have to put new powerful positive thoughts into your head? It is not always other people who are at fault for our life situation; sometimes we are fault by letting all the negativity from others INSIDE US.

ASK YOURSELF! LOOK DEEP into yourself. Admit it to yourself and start to work on yourself.

And every person and every situation we have had in our lives wasn't there accidentally. Some of them were a blessing and some of them were a lesson. It's depends on us whether we want to stay in the "victim" state of being our whole lives or whether we are ready to change it. Sometimes, if we want to become a better person we must first to make big changes in ourselves, not in others. We have difficult lives because we make easy choices.

If we want to have easy lives, sometimes we have to make some difficult choices. The choice to change our subconscious mind, the choice to change ourselves, not to wait for others to change. Stop waiting, my lovely, and do something!

PLEASE 🙏

We are waiting for the perfect relationship, for the perfect job, for the big money to come to us in order be happy or fulfilled. If we don't change ourselves, my lovely, and be grateful and happy in this moment for everything we have, there are two options that could happen if we got everything we ever wished for. First option: We wouldn't be happy and fulfilled even if we had all these things, because we were concentrated on what we didn't have our whole lives, and even if we had everything, there would be always be something that we didn't have, and we would think about that, not about what we have.

And the second option: we will not see that all these things that we always wanted are around us, because we unconsciously don't BELIEVE that we deserve that all these good things come into our lives, based on our past experiences and based on our current negative thoughts, my lovely. When were you nice to yourself the last time, my lovely? Have you sometimes said to yourself,

I am so happy today?

I am thankful for everything I have?

I am blessed?

I am worthy?

I am enough?

If you didn't, then do that my Lovely and be honest and gentle to yourself my lovely!

You deserve that.

And shift your looking at yourself from negative to positive, for example; Let's say you have an interview for your dream job. Be honest to yourself and look at your thoughts. They go like this:

Do I look good?

Are there any other candidates today?

Are they better qualified than me?

Am I good enough for this job?

I definitely cannot get this job.

What shall I do If I don't get this job?

Everybody will say that I am a loser. Again!

And how many of you, my lovely, would think before going to the same interview some positive thoughts or scenarios? For example:

I can get this job now!

I believe in myself!

I will go in, I will do my best, and I will get this job!

Maybe 20% of you.

This book is not for you, my lovely!

I am speaking here about the majority of you, for the 80% who are full of fear, doubts and anger, and you still think that it is because of your outer world, No, my lovely,

LOOK DEEP INSIDE!

In another words, you don't believe that we you were born for the good things in life, and you always begin with the worst possible scenario, my lovely. I don't know where that comes from, my lovely, maybe your parents got divorced and you felt as a child that it was because of you. Maybe your Dad or your Mom were angry with you and told you that you are never going to make it in life, maybe your Mom left you as a small child and you cannot get over that. I really don't know your personal story, but this lack of confidence and self-belief commonly come from our closest environment, and we have to recreate ourselves, but first do something that you never did before, my lovely, and that is to FORGIVE THEM!

FORGIVE EVERYONE WHO DID SOMETHING "BAD" TO YOU IN YOUR LIFE!

You are forgiving them not because of them, my lovely, you are forgiving because of you! If you don't forgive them, you're going to suffer, my lovely, you'll suffer because someone else did something to you! THEY WON'T! They will not suffer for something which they did.

That is the same as if you swallow a poison pill and you expect someone else to die! No, my lovely, you are dying INSIDE.

PLEASE DO IT, FORGIVE THEM DEEP IN YOUR HEART FOR YOU OWN GOOD, MY LOVELY!

And always keep an eye on your negative unconscious thinking and do your best to not respond to these negative thoughts. Because we sometimes respond to these thought as if there were another person INSIDE US, and we waste our energy on the worst possible scenario that could happen. And guess what? It will happen, my lovely!

What you need to do is to look at your negative thoughts as if they were an uninvited visitor who you can see coming to your door, but you don't want to let him INSIDE your house (your head), so try not responding to him, just let him go, without reactions, especially without emotional reactions.

Such thoughts consume our energy, and instead of turning it into something positive we accept the entry of this negative information that is not true and acts as if it were.

The truth is, we are born to be what we decide to be, we have the capacity to create miracles, to create a life full of joy in every single moment, to do work full of passion where we don't need to wait for the weekend to relax. And if we haven't achieved that until this point in our lives, we are capable of reprogramming ourselves, especially when see that we have unconsciously chosen some other people's program. We are the one and only species or beings in the whole world, my lovely, who spend more time in the past and in the future than in the present moment.

We are the only beings on the planet who are capable of making everything that has happened to us in our lives look as if we were the victims of unfavorable circumstances. And based on these unfavorable circumstances and things that have happened to us, and what people say about us, we create our beliefs about ourselves, wrong beliefs that our abilities are limited. I am talking about this broken belief system, my lovely! We are not present in the now, we judge yesterday and we have doubts about tomorrow.

Then where we are living, my lovely?

In some three-dimensional world created from yesterday, now and tomorrow? That means we are everywhere and nowhere at the same time! That is the same as if you worked in three jobs at the same time, my lovely. You can't do one job properly if you work on three at the same time. We have to get rid of something, my lovely, immediately. First we must get rid of our past. Let it go. NOW! As I said, everything in our past was either a blessing or a lesson for us.

The second thing is to treat the future which we wish for ourselves as if it were already present fact. NOW! In the present moment.

And the third and most important thing is to put a little BELIEF into the whole process, a little more BELIEF, my lovely. Combine the present moment and the future into ONE, into ONE EMOTION. And the world will open up for you, my lovely. The new one, the real one, INSIDE YOU!

What you can also do to get rid of your old negative thoughts and habits is to use good positive thoughts and habits. For every negative thought put two positive thoughts INTO YOUR HEAD. How? Very simple, with affirmations.

Instead of saying to yourself, "I am ugly," say to yourself a hundred times a day, "I am beautiful!"

Instead to saying to yourself, "I am stupid," say to yourself a hundred times a day, "I am smart."

Change all your negative thoughts about YOURSELF into positive ones like:

I am capable, I am good enough, I was born for great things, I attract only good things, only good comes from me, only good comes to me, I am not afraid, and the list goes on and on! And repeat that hundreds of times, every day. Even if you don't have so many negative thoughts, repeat positive ones over and over again.

Our unconscious MIND or subconscious MIND only understands repetition, pictures or visualization. Our unconscious MIND is stronger and has more capacity to produce what it wants to achieve than our conscious MIND.

That's why it is our target.

Here is where all our BELIEFS are hidden about what is possible in life for us, and what is not possible. In our unconscious or subconscious mind, my lovely!

If you can change your negative beliefs about what is possible for YOU in your unconscious mind, then the sky is your limit! And as I said, our unconscious MIND understands pictures, affirmations and visualization. That's why you should have a clear picture in your head of where you want to be in five years. Assume this is already reality and keep the FEELING close to you every single day. Then repeat your affirmations over and over again. I really mean over and over again, hundreds of times a day!

Don't be disappointed when you see that you are not there after a few tries. That's why a lot of people don't BELIEVE that this actually works, but it's nothing but constant work on yourself, on your way of thinking. Work on your way of acting and work on the way you look at yourself and work on what you want to happen, not on what you are afraid of, and you will see, my lovely. It's a daily job, and if you put in the effort you'll see that it actually works. And regarding what you want to attract or achieve, it is very important not to ask questions about how it is going to come to you, or when it is going to come to you. Just keep that nice feeling that it is already happening to, keep it very close to you and BELIEVE.

Every day.

Every hour.

Every minute.

Try it.

Before you start to judge, try it.

Don't be afraid about being judged by others. If you're afraid don't tell anybody that you are doing this, and take five minutes a day only for yourself. Doubters are all around us. Open your heart and trust. Believe, my lovely, because we are changing your belief system here. This is one of the crucial factors, because this is the place where all your dreams are going to be CREATED OR where they have already DIED! Why, my lovely?

Because you are too focused on your outside reality, reality created only by material things, and nobody LOOKS INSIDE, my lovely, DEEP INSIDE in ourselves!

LOOK DEEP INSIDE!

And don't look for excuses: that you have no time, that you are going through a rough time, or that it is too good to be true, this are only excuses and if you say, "I'll do that, but…" be aware that everything you say after "but" makes no difference anymore.

But is the world's best-known word for excuses.

I would like to read a book, BUT I don't have time!

I would like to quit my shitty job, BUT I am afraid!

I would love to have my own apartment, BUT it's not possible now!

So no buts, just try it, my lovely!

Before you go to sleep.

Imagine something you want to have. Don't think about the bad things that already happened to you that day, IMAGINE, recreate the child INSIDE you and assume you already have it in your hands. Remember that feeling. And stay close to this feeling every time you think about this thing. Bad thoughts will come; our ego mind has to do something, but stay close to this feeling and you will see.

Miracles are going to start happening to you.

Miracles happen only if you BELIEVE in them. Reprogram your BELIEF system because BELIEFS are nothing more than decisions, and if you made a decision a long time ago that you are not good enough, make a new decision today and start to believe that you ARE good enough. Believe me, believe yourself, believe HIM. If you've lost your belief, let's bring it back, together! That is what it's all about, believing that everything is possible for you. Or for your lovely family.

Keep this picture in your mind of what you want to manifest.

I heard a story that airplanes are off course 75 % of the time, but the pilot brings them back, over and over again. Your plane (life) is going to be of course too, but you have the power to bring it back. Over and over again! You are the pilot of your plane.

I know, my lovely we are conditioned to think differently especially when our whole life have been told to be afraid of GOD, that only rich people get richer, and poor people get poorer, that we need to have a secure job and to not ask a lot of questions because we can get fired, that only the people with connections make money, but not us, we are "normal" people and nothing more! I AM speaking from my own experience my Lovely, have you heard such things and maybe even worse?

It is up to us to get ready and prepare ourselves for a hell of a job and start cleaning out our subconscious mind, because everything is memorized there.

But don't be afraid and take action, my lovely. Do not let yourself be driven, take control of your life.

For example, if you use affirmations by saying to yourself, "Today, everything good comes from me." Then take action and do some good things that day, try it, make the effort.

If you say, "Today, all good comes to me," take action and think about some nice things that you want to happen, not about some bad things that you don't want to happen to you. Make the effort.

If you want to say, for example, today I see only the good in everything that happens to me, make the effort and really see only the good in everything what has just happened to you.

I can speak from my own experience, or you can read other spiritual books or watch videos on YouTube, but you and only you have to take action, and for everything you learn, you have to put in the effort, nobody can do it for you. Not me nor any other author.

Now that you know that you are not your thoughts, and not your body, now that you know that you are not your EGO MIND, and that you are pure awareness or pure consciousness, that you are the witness who looks through your eyes, that you are the light, that you are One with all beings, and most importantly that you are One with your Source, connected in every single moment to HIM, now tell me please what stands in the way of you creating the life that you always wanted to live?

Are your thoughts saying to you that it won't work? We already agreed that we are not our thoughts. Or is your body saying you are too old? That it's too late now?

There are thousands of stories of people who found their true self and passion in their late 50s or 60s, and we have already agreed that we are not our bodies. Is your EGO MIND telling you, you can't make it?

Of course, it is doing its job of over-controlling, and it does that very well, but it only wants to pull our attention in the wrong direction. But we already agreed that we are not our EGOs. Then what is stopping you from starting step by step? It is only your BELIEF system, but don't worry, we're going to fix it, together, but please do something before we start to work on your BELIEF system. Be honest and admit to yourself when you brush your teeth in the morning, admit that you put up a big "Stop" sign in your head without accepting everything we spoke about as if it was about YOU.

Now be brave enough to take this sign and throw it away with all your strength, and prepare yourself for miracles. Keep your house (mind) open, open for a new you, the real you, the pure unconditional you.

In the same moment when something INSIDE recognizes the truth and you feel the butterflies in your stomach, be ready for even more resistance from your EGO MIND, and be ready for the worst storm of thoughts, negative ones of course, to come to you. Your EGO MIND will not give up so easily. It is comfortable until you recognize that you are not it. Then it becomes stronger and stronger. You know that you will always be one step ahead if you are aware that this negative voice is not yours, even though it sometimes seems like yours. Just don't listen to it.

You will have good days and bad days. Sometimes it will look as if it has control over you again, your ego mind, that it is stronger than you. And it is not a problem if you lose some battles, if you have some bad days, but you have to win the war, my lovely, and if you are aware in every single moment that you are not it, you will win the war. Definitely.

Don't give up. Ever! Keep pushing every single day. When it is under threat it has ideas that are more than crazy. Bad ideas.

In the book *The Fear* by Kosta Petrov, he explains the EGO as the fear in him, and in the same moment as he said to it, "My friend, the time has finally come to end this friendship", the EGO, or the fear in this case, was itself so scared that it would be left by one of its clients that it became very strong, and then this voice or the EGO told him to not eat anything because he would get sick, and not to go to sleep because he would not wake up in the morning, and every night before he went to bed, Kosta kissed the picture of his family because a strong voice told him that he would die. This happened to him over and over again and every single day, my lovely. This is just another true example of how innovative our EGO can be, only to keep us close to it.

Don't be afraid, even when it gets stronger, then you will be even more sure that this voice only wants to make us scared. Wake up the divine in yourself. And feel your divine INSIDE every time it attacks you. Stick to the good in you, ignore the bad, say to yourself, "I have a greater purpose in this world, and I am not giving you my attention, my EGO friend."

> *"Be the change that you wish to see in the world."*
> \- Mahatma Gandhi

I am the change that I want to see in the world. I am trying every single day. I am giving my best. I am writing my book on my boring night shifts and I know it's a very brave move because there are going to be all types of comments about my book, but I don't care anymore, my lovely.

I know DEEP INSIDE that I AM doing the right thing and that's the only thing that matters.

Be the change.

Give your best.

Stand up and make changes, do the work and you are going to feel better. If you feel better everybody around you will also feel better. This is basically doing nothing and achieving everything. From the outside it looks as if you were doing nothing, but the real work is done within you. Make the effort and you will see the changes.

You will become less judgmental about other people.

You will become more self-aware.

You will be able to control your emotions.

You will be able to look at and also control your thoughts.

You will become FEARLESS.

And you will see there are no coincidences in your life; you will see that everything happens for a reason. You will be able to be still and you will know that you are GOD. Sounds scary?

Of course it sounds scary for our ego mind, because when you are under the control of your EGO your life is all about you, and when you finally feel HIS presence in your heart and you realize that you are ONE WITH YOUR GOD, ONE WITH YOUR SOURCE, that your life isn't about you any more, then your life has become about serving others. First LOOK DEEP INSIDE, my lovely, and then be still and the answer will come to you.

You can read the sentence, "Be still and know that I am GOD," more than a hundred times in the book which was found in the hands of Elvis Presley when they found him dead in his bedroom in Graceland.

The Impersonal life

Joseph Benner

This book was first published anonymously in 1914 and is known as one of the first teachings at that time about knowing that we are ONE with GOD. The author had a very important role at that time in the government and he didn't want to publish it in his own name, because 100 years ago this type of teaching went against everything people believed in the field of religion and also in general.

For a long time, the sentence "Be still and know that I am God" was one of my affirmations, and it still is today. But the question is, why I am mentioning it now?

To show you that these affirmations work, and so you are not afraid to ASK your GOD, and to not be afraid of HIM, to FEEL HIM, and BELIEVE HIM. By being still and knowing that HE is HERE, in YOU. As I said earlier, I started to use affirmations, and almost one year ago I wrote something on a piece of paper, something that at that time seemed to be right to me, but appeared to sound crazy to everybody else I knew at that time. It was:

Dear God, please inspire me to write a book about how I can find YOU in myself, and to inspire others to also find YOU in themselves.

Thank you!

I wrote that one year ago in my native language. Now it is December and I started to write my book two months ago, and it is almost finished. On the night shifts of my "dream" job! I knew HE could also speak and read Macedonian.☺

Be still and know you are GOD, my lovely. And you can also feel HIM, believe HIM, know HIM, my lovely, just pay attention DEEP INSIDE. This piece of paper was in my wallet for a year, and it is still in my wallet, and I became inspired two months ago. It works, my lovely. Be still and know you are GOD!

Ask with an open heart and clear intention and you will receive it, sooner or later. Be still and know that I am GOD!

Repeat that to yourself. If you are worried about other people's opinions don't tell them what you are doing, work on yourself secretly, as I did. But when I saw that this actually works I wanted to share it with the world. I just want to help! And be yourself my lovely, do not let negative people to pull you into their negative and selfish world. Be less judgmental and more self-aware, because when people say bad things about you to your face or behind your back they are actually speaking about themselves, not about you.

> *"How people treat you is their karma. How you react is yours."*
>
> - Wayne Dyer

You and only you have the key to your INNER world where everything happens. Don't let everything inside, especially not the negative opinions of other people. I know, my lovely, you will become a very boring person when you do not judge, when you don't complain, when you accept the present moment just the way it is, when you don't want to speak about your bad past and your unpredictable future any more, but you will be a boring person only in the eyes of people who are negative and always complaining, not in the eyes of people who really know you, not in the eyes of the people who care about you and who love you most! In their eyes you will be the proof that you can change YOURSELF, but only if you really DEEPLY want to. Don't wait for the world to change in order that you can change, don't wait for the circumstances to change in order for you to change. Change yourself first, your way of thinking and acting, my lovely, and don't waste time!

We spend more than 50% of our time complaining, speaking about others and not being satisfied with the present moment, always looking backwards or forwards. Imagine what you can achieve if you transform this energy into something that you love. Reprogram your belief system, my lovely, and the magic will happen to you. Don't always wait for others to believe in you so that you can start to believe in yourself!

Yes, I know, we all want to be told that we are the best, that we are the smartest or the prettiest, but sometimes we are not, especially in the eyes of others, no matter how much effort we make, because we all see the world with different eyes. That's normal and ok. We don't need to hate each other or kill each other only because we have different opinions about something or different views of each other. But unfortunately that has become normal.

For everybody to be against everybody. To live in fear has become something very normal.

Turn on your TV and watch the news, my lovely!

Or you don't need to watch the news, look around you. In your company for example, two people with two different opinions are not the best of friends, are they? Or even worse, if you don't agree with the majority of your co-workers, you don't fit in. If you "only" want to do your job and go at home without saying nasty things about others, things that are not even true, then something is wrong with you!

You have to say something bad about the colleague who just left 20 minutes ago. If not, you are weird, is something wrong with you? No everything is ok with you my Lovely.

We all believe in something, my lovely! In some higher power. You can call it whatever you want. Divine power, soul, spirit or whatever you want to call it. Buddha, Brahman, Jesus, Allah. It makes no difference. Tell me which one of them taught us 200 years or 2000 years ago to hate each other or to kill each other? Name it? Who?

No-one, my lovely.

They each taught us in different ways, but they taught us to respect each other, to love each other, no matter who or in which GOD we believe, no matter what you look like, which skin color you have, or in which culture you were raised. It makes no difference!

We are all ONE.

We all came from nothing and we will go back to nothing, without having the opportunity to take anything with us. Without having the opportunity to come back in this form again, ever! If we only had this one sentence in our heads every single day, we wouldn't be worried about most of the self-created and imagined problems that we have. We have this limited time to experience life and then we go back to our source. And we use this time to hate each other, to kill each other?

Well done, my fellow human.

Remember, the various GODS, in which we all believe, don't kill each other, they don't hate each other. We kill our fellow humans, we hate each other, and in that way we stop each other growing and becoming a better version of ourselves. We and we alone!

Wake up my fellow humans.

If you are not willing to change something in your own life and to help yourself to be a better person it's ok, it's your choice, but stop behaving badly to your friends, your neighbors or even worse to your lovely family. That's against every religion, every belief, every normal way of thinking. Try something new, try a new path, don't always follow the old patterns.

Try to look differently at the world. Start to BELIEVE that we can make a difference.

I know you can't make a difference alone, neither can I, but if every single one of us makes an effort and we give our best on a daily basis for the good of ourselves and others, we can definitely make a difference. Together, my lovely! Don't ever think that you are not worth it, don't ever feel ashamed or bad if you don't fit into this system of perfection today, my lovely, if your stomach is too big, if your skin color is different, if the God in which you believe is different to that of your neighbor, if your opinions are not same as those of others. Never try to be loved in order to be accepted by society, just be the way you are, be yourself because you are more than perfect and beautiful, you are pure unconditional LOVE created by HIM. Know DEEP INSIDE that YOU are ONE with your creator and you have big role to play in this world. It is only matter of time until you find your true self and purpose in this world, my lovely!

That's why you should start with gratitude, my lovely. Be grateful.

Be grateful for what you have, fight and give your best for more in life, but first be aware and grateful for what you have. For example, my lovely:

Let us say you are doing some good things for your best friend and you are helping him as much as you can. Sometimes more, sometimes less, but you are helping him over and over again. And he is always unsatisfied, he is complaining all the time, he is saying, "Ok, nice of you, but you could do more," and he always expects more from you.

Would you do something for him again, my lovely?

Would you help him if you see that he is always unhappy and he wants more and more without being thankful for what you have already done for him? Of course not. I wouldn't either. It's the same thing with the universe. With GOD!

We are asking always only for more and more without considering giving something back, or even worse, without even being grateful for what HE has already given us. And when HE stops giving to us, we blame HIM, we don't ask ourselves where the problem is. We are used to blaming everyone else when we don't get what we want. Everything begins with you, or rather, WITHIN you.

I had to go through all this my lovely, always unsatisfied, always in the past, which I thought was the worst past which one could ever have, or in the future, creating all these bad scenarios in my head that something bad will happen to me or to my family, always blaming others for my life "situation", but I became aware of that, and with constant work on myself now I have a different MINDset.

I am not saying that I am now a Zen master without negative thoughts and always at peace!

No, I am not, but I give my best every single day to be aware of my unconscious thoughts, to let them go if some bad thought comes up or to remove them if they are already inside, and to meditate. If I can't do something good for someone, I do them good by doing nothing bad to them. I am conscious of the power of the words I AM, even when I feel weak I say I AM strong, because I no longer want to use GOD's name for negative things, and it's work, my lovely. I changed my BELIEF system from nothing is possible to everything is possible, and if I could do that, you can do it, too. That's why I always write I AM in capital letters here, so you get it into your unconscious MIND and use it in an appropriate way. But that is everyday work, taking place behind the work you do, the obligations that you have or the negative environment in which people only believe in what they see, taste or touch. Behind the curtains is the main event. The real job is WITHIN you. Work on yourself, my lovely.

At the beginning when I started this adventure after reading the ONE book I didn't think there were so many people interested in this topic of the EGO and finding YOURSELF. But I was surprised how many people struggle with this unseen "enemy", with this inner conflict between the good and the bad, between GOD and EGO, between known and unknown, between fear and love, and I realized that when I received a gift from my wife. It was a ticket for an Eckhart Tolle event in Salzburg.

One of my favorite spiritual teachers was coming here, only 200km away from us, and my wife didn't want me to miss this opportunity, so she bought me a ticket and I was so happy about that. I went to Salzburg alone because someone had to stay at home with our angels, and as I said I was surprised how many people were looking for an answer to their inner problems and conflicts. There were people with families, people with small children, successful people, celebrities, and every single one of them was looking for a solution for the internal wars they had. There were more than 5000 people and they came there only to hear a little wisdom first hand.

It was at very special evening for me.

I learned a lot that evening. I learned a lot about the value of the present moment, about detachment from the past and avoiding worries about the future, and Eckhart's personal story is also very inspiring for me. In that moment, I knew DEEP INSIDE that I would also stand on the stage one day and talk to an audience about my spiritual awakening and help others to be more self-aware and conscious in their everyday lives. If I could shift my consciousness, everyone can do it, my lovely. Don't be afraid and take action.

Fifty percent of our problems are solved only if we admit and we are aware that we have a problem. If you don't accept your fears and problems the only one who can lose is you. Have faith and do not be afraid. Everything is possible with GOD. BELIEVE, my lovely. The one who sets boundaries in your head is you, not GOD. It is only you with your limited beliefs who sets your boundaries. We have so many examples of how true miracles have happened to our fellow humans, not only today but throughout history. The only question is, do you BELIEVE that miracles can happen to you or not?

Or aren't you brave enough to IMAGINE a better future for yourself and your loved ones, and not to be disappointed when the miracles you wished for are not already there in the same moment you wished for them. Be the small child again who has great faith that Santa will bring him or her toys, but not today, not tomorrow, not when he or she wants, but when the right time comes. They are not disappointed when you tell them, "Be patient, Honey, Santa is on his way with your gifts." They truly and DEEPLY BELIEVE that he is on his way with their toys! Be the small child INSIDE even if you are an adult OUTSIDE. Keep asking questions every single day and imagine how it would be to have everything you asked and wished for, and BELIEVE that it is on its way to you.

It's never too late, my lovely. I also had to rediscover the child in myself in my late thirties.

Until I came into contact with CONVERSATIONS WITH GOD, I thought "That's it, Jane.

Now you are married and you have children you have to stay in the same job and wait to die." I didn't dare to ask for or imagine more. I had been taught that that's how it is.

To IMAGINE working with love and passion? No way!!

I talked to my wife about my belief that life isn't about this endless routine: wake up, go to work, come home after work, play a little with the kids, eat and go to bed. Like robots. I told her that something bigger was hiding here, that we are not just born to survive, that we are born to LIVE OUR FULL POTENTIAL, but even while I was saying that to her I didn't dare to IMAGINE because I didn't BELIEVE DEEP INSIDE that it was possible for me.

To IMAGINE to live in abundance and not in a state of lack? No way, my lovely. In my late thirties I also had to learn to recreate my IMAGINATION.

If I was capable of creating bad scenarios INSIDE, what was stopping me from rebuilding them with good outcomes? Now I know that I was stopping myself, my EGO mind was stopping me. You can also stop creating misery INSIDE YOURSELF and rewrite your story. Start with more FAITH, more BELIEF and more AWARENESS of the fact that HE hears us when we speak to HIM, and HE will respond to us when we are ready to RECEIVE THE ANSWER.

There is one line in CONVERSATIONS WITH GOD which says more than a thousand words.

GOD says to Neale,

"The question is not to whom I AM speaking, the question is who is listening?"

That's why when you start to ask questions, be still, present and listen. Maybe you don't BELIEVE now, but he will answer you sooner or later. Change all your old beliefs about yourself, about life, about what is possible is for you and what is not. Go beyond your analytical mind, beyond your negative thoughts, beyond your fears. Go beyond all the boundaries that you have created for yourself. And there is your power, your strength and your source of creativity.

To create a better you, a happier you, a healthier you, a wealthier you.

You can shine in every aspect of your life, my lovely. You are worthy of living this life in the way you want to live it. DEEP INSIDE nobody wants to life a life full of fear and lack. Although we know DEEP INSIDE that this is true, why do we let our environment brainwash our MINDS with all the negativity and limited beliefs around us?

Brainwash yourself before the world brainwashes you!

Do not be so preoccupied with your physical form, but be preoccupied with what is really happening INSIDE YOU, and reprogram yourself, brainwash yourself for success, wealth and happiness before the world brainwashes you with fear, lack and anxiety! In this and in other ways which I described earlier, you can win the first battle with "your" negative thoughts and realize that they aren't actually yours. Let them go just go through you. Do not stop them and keep them in you. They are not yours!

Please, my lovely.

Try to see yourself with the loving eyes with which your creator sees you. See yourself from another point of view and be gentle to yourself, you deserve it. Then direct your attention INSIDE you, still your mind even for a few minutes every day and try to just Be.

Try to understand that a higher power is INSIDE YOU, not outside somewhere, but INSIDE YOU. Use every single moment that you have to focus your attention INSIDE, my lovely. In so many ways you can connect WITHIN YOU. You will realize that you are not alone and you are not separate from your SOURCE.

You are ONE in your heart with HIM.

And before sharing one last teaching that helped me to go beyond my old BELIEF system I want to tell you that I truly hope that TOGETHER we have already changed some limited beliefs about you, my lovely! BY sharing my true personal story, I DEEPLY wanted YOU to change your beliefs about yourself by changing your perception of things that have already happened and the things that will yet happen in your life, in order for YOU to start

OVER AGAIN to BELIEVE IN YOURSELF, TO BELIEVE IN HIM and to BELIEVE THAT MIRACLES ARE OUR REALITY!

"IF YOU CHANGE THE WAY YOU LOOK AT THINGS, THE THINGS YOU LOOK AT CHANGE"
Wayne Dyer

As a child, I am sure you had the BELIEF that you were not loved and appreciated as much as you thought you should be, but that was only your perception of things. With my last teaching it will become clearer that if we only change our perception of things, we can also change the BELIEF that you as a child were not loved and appreciated enough. You had the BELIEF that you are this negative voice in your head, now you know YOU ARE NOT!

You had the BELIEF that you are your ego mind, now you know YOU ARE NOT!

You had the BELIEF that you are your negative thoughts, now you know YOU ARE NOT!

You had the BELIEF that you are what others think about you, now you know YOU ARE NOT!

You had the BELIEF that your past is responsible for why your life is not working in the present moment, now you know IT'S NOT YOUR PAST'S FAULT, IT'S YOUR FAULT FOR NOT LETTING YOUR PAST GO.

You had the BELIEF that you cannot influence your future, now you know YOU CAN.

BY LETTING YOUR PAST GO, BEING AWARE OF THE PRESENT MOMENT, AND FROM THE PRESENT MOMENT CREATING THE FUTURE THAT YOU WANT TO MANIFEST!

As I said our subconscious mind can only be changed with repetition. Don't let other people create your BELIEFS about what is possible in YOUR LIFE!

PLEASE my lovely, do not let other people's opinions create your BELIEFS about yourself.

I made this mistake, please you don't do that!

There will always be negative people around us, but the question is how we are going to react to them, not how we are going to change them, I had to change MYSELF also and by changing MYSELF I started to react differently to my negative environment, and the BELIEF in myself slowly came back, but it wasn't always like that.

I also had limited beliefs, and when you live all your life with limited beliefs you will have limited success in your life.

And limited points of view.

And limited expectations of yourself.

And limited standards.

And worst of all: a limited life.

I can live with knowing that I didn't make anything of my life, but I cannot live with the knowledge that I didn't do anything to try to change it. That's why I have said hundreds of times: if you see something is wrong in your life, first try to find the solution in yourself, not in others. And the solution to the problem will reveal itself around you if you show a willingness to change yourself.

I was ready to change myself, especially when I read CONVERSATIONS WITH GOD. I knew that I didn't want to be the same person any more, and I opened up for a new way of thinking, for a new way of seeing myself, and the world INSIDE me opened itself automatically, and that's why I am sharing with you every single experience that I had, and every single story I read that helped me to be a better person today.

Now let's go back once more to the period of time when all this actually started, in our childhood, the most important period of time where we unconsciously created a lot of negative BELIEFS about ourselves and others and since then have unconsciously used them throughout our lives. This really helped me. Hopefully it will help you too, my lovely!

And with this teaching I come to the end of my experience of how I was able to reprogram myself into the person that I wanted to become. You, my lovely, can also reprogram yourself to live a life with all your potential and without boundaries anymore.

This is one of the teachings of Morty Lefkoe.

He is known as founder of the Lefkoe method. This method is world famous and tried and tested. He helps others to change or remove the negative beliefs about themselves which they are aware of, even when people are not aware that their negative beliefs are actually the main problem why they couldn't progress in their lives.

He says that we as adults all have core beliefs about ourselves and some are positive and some are negative. And they are: life is not too difficult or life is difficult, I am good enough or I am not good enough, I am important or I am not important. These are our basic beliefs about ourselves.

But he says most people form some of these negative core beliefs about themselves as children in their first years of life during interaction with their parents, environment, etc. For example, I am not worthy, I can't do that, I am powerless, I am the reason why Mom and Dad argue, and as he said, these negative beliefs about ourselves are created especially in the first 6-7 years of our lives in interactions with our parents based on the fact that one of our parents was not there, or both of them were not there, or they were there but emotionally they were not present. We create a belief in our childhood that their physical or mental absence is because of us, and we create a belief that we are not good enough, that something is wrong with us, and that's why my parents behave like this to me, that's why my Mom or my Dad are not at home, that's why Mom and Dad got divorced, because of me. And we create negative beliefs about ourselves based on what we see and hear as children, because our conscious mind isn't developed enough to have our own opinion about ourselves and that's why everything we hear and see gets stuck in our subconscious minds, which, as we said earlier, are responsible for 95% of our functioning, which includes breathing, the beating of the heart, the functioning of the brain, and extends to thinking, acting, behaving and believing, and the list goes on and on.

And for me it makes sense, because who today is concessly concentrated on his breathing, or on his heart beating, I mean consciously? Nobody, my lovely, and we think that happens normally, spontaneously, but nothing happens spontaneously in our bodies, and when we think about what runs the machinery inside us, the answer is simple. It's our subconscious or unconscious mind which is our target if we want to change our BELIEF system.

Here is something from Joe Dispenza's teachings about how our subconscious mind controls 95-99% of what happens in our lives, and this perfectly matches Lefkoe's teaching about why we as children created the negative BELIEFS that we have now as adults.

Joe says that in the first two years of the child's life their brain waves are basically in delta: they sleep with open eyes, and as they come into interaction with their environment their brain waves change to theta. Theta is a wave pattern where we often have mystical experiences, but in the first six years of a child's life they are completely in their subconscious mind because that is what all their wave patterns do, and as result of that all their attention is on their emotions. From the sixth until the ninth year of the child's life, their wave patterns change from alpha to beta. Beta is the analytical mind which is able to differentiate between the conscious and the subconscious mind. As small children we hadn't yet developed this analytical mind to review things that have happened. In this early stage of life, we experienced the world around us subconsciously, only through our emotions.

If we don't change our BELIEFS, and something happens to you now as an adult, and exactly the same thing happened to you when you were a 5-6-year-old boy or girl, you are going to react just like the 5-6-year-old child, because you remember your emotion and your subconscious remembers how you felt at that time.

I know from my own experience.

And that's why I wrote at the beginning of this chapter that this is the most important one if you want to change yourself, my lovely. Now let's go back on Lefkoe's teaching.

He says that until the time comes when we to go to school, and that is until the 7th year of our lives, we spend most of our time with our parents and may hear some things that we as children weren't supposed to hear, like our parents having arguments about money, and we instantly create a belief that money is something bad because it is the reason why Mom and Dad are having an argument. Or Mom and Dad have an argument in front of the child about its sister or brother, and the child creates a belief that his or her sister or brother are the cause of the argument and that it is his or her fault. Or the Dad or Mom say some unpleasant words to their child every time it does some stupid thing or makes a mistake at home, and the child creates a negative belief about itself in that same moment: that it is not good enough.

And he says the list of examples of creating limited negative beliefs about ourselves and about a lot of things in our lives goes on and on and that these beliefs are created unconsciously in the first seven years of our lives. Beliefs that are going to dictate our whole life without us even being aware of it.

And then he says that when we start to go to school and we try – with these limited negative beliefs about ourselves which we picked up from our family – to manage our "problems" at school, our problems with our school friends, or with our teachers, what happens then? We are going to have some difficult times because we already think that we are not good enough, we can't do this or we can't do that, or we are not good enough to have friends. And we feel bad about that, or we feel afraid every time when some issue comes up because our beliefs about ourselves are already negative.

An important part of his teaching is where he asks us to go back in time to see the small child in some of these not so pleasant situations, and he asks us to describe how it feels to think that we are not good enough for our own parents.

And we all say, of course, bad! It feels bad.

Ok, he says that is a view from a child's perspective, and it is one possible interpretation of your parents' behavior. Let's now try to see the situation as an adult. What could be another possible interpretation of the same situation? He says, let's say for example that your parents were just busy, that their behavior had nothing to do with you as a child; maybe you were the most important thing in their lives but they were just busy and stressed. That could be one interpretation.

Another interpretation could be they were dealing with their stress in their own way and that it had nothing to do with you as a child, and they just had financial problems, and they didn't know how to handle the situation, and that's why they were nervous and angry with everybody around themselves, including you as their child. Another interpretation could be that they were trying to provide you with everything you needed, and they were working very hard, and that's why they were not there, sometimes emotionally and sometimes physically. Then he says that we can see that they are several possible interpretations of one situation and that maybe it had nothing to do with us as children, and that what we thought was the truth when we were children isn't actually the truth at all; it is one of many possible truths.

And now the most important thing: he says close your eyes and be once again the small you, see your Dad is not here and your Mom is here, but she is not here emotionally, and you feel unimportant once again, can you see this feeling?

And we all say, "Yes, I can see this feeling."

Now open your eyes and describe this feeling to me, how it looks like?

And of course I cannot describe this feeling because this feeling exists only in my mind and cannot be described. We can describe something that really exists in our reality, like a pencil for example, but we cannot describe something which doesn't exist. This feeling doesn't have a form, a real form. He says that this BELIEF is something that we created in our CHILD minds, that actually doesn't exist as a form.

And that's why we cannot get rid of some BELIEFS, because we think we have saw them. And we think we saw it hundreds of times, and that's why we think it is the truth. No, it's not the truth, my lovely! No, we didn't see it, we created it, we created these negative beliefs in our minds!

I finally figured it out.

This teaching helped me a to see that as a child I and only I created a belief about myself that I was not worthy, and that everything I did was not good enough in my parents' eyes. This teaching showed me that I was and I AM still the creator of my own BELIEFS. I and nobody else. Their behavior in relation to their own problems at that time had nothing to do with me as their child. Their not knowing how to deal with their problems and our problems at that time didn't have anything to do with how they felt about us. They loved us and cared about us so much, just as we love our children today, and we think that we are the best parents in the world. But at the end of the day they will create their own beliefs about us as parents and about themselves, certainly not based on our thinking that we are the best, but based on their perception of us as parents.

I know I was a good boy and I am certainly the same good boy in their eyes today, even if I alone created a bad picture in my head about myself and I thought they had the same picture in their heads, too. I also created a bad opinion of my Dad based on what was told to me as a child and later also as a teenager, but he wasn't actually even half as bad as some people close to me tried to make out.

Sorry Dad for creating an image of you in my head, something that you were not. I shouldn't have created a picture of you based on that what others were saying about you, I shouldn't have created a picture of you based only on those few moments when you couldn't control your emotions. Sorry, I was just a kid. You should be proud of yourself; you did the best you could and thank you for everything.

Sorry Mom for creating in my head the Mom that you were supposed to be and not accepting the Mom that you were, the best Mom in the world. You should also be proud of yourself Mom, and thanks for everything from the bottom of my heart.

You my dear Parents gave me more than I could understand, You gave me the FREEDOM to BE GO and DO what I ever wanted to, YOU GAVE ME WINGS TO FLY. Thank you.

A lot of the time, maybe 90% of the time, you are really a good parent, my lovely, but in the remaining 10% of the time you let yourself be controlled by your emotions when you have money problems or you lose your job. Then you may say some not so pleasant things to your kids, and in these moments of stress they can create negative beliefs about themselves and also a bad image of you.

A BELIEF that may stay close to them for a long, long time.

A BELIEF that can have major effects in every area of their lives. Until they become aware that what they created in their heads does not actually exist in reality.

A BELIEF that they are responsible for your unhappiness or for your bad financial situation.

My lovely parents, children aren't responsible for anything. We as adults have a perception of ourselves, just like our children, but the only difference is we can change this perception, children can't.

Not alone at least. But with your help, my lovely parents, they certainly CAN. We ALL live in a perception of a perception of ourselves, my lovely!

I think you think I am not good enough, and I don't feel good enough in your presence.

I think you think I am responsible for something, and I feel responsible in your presence.

I think you think I am not smart, and I feel stupid in your presence.

I think you think I that I am not beautiful and I don't feel beautiful in your presence.

My lovely parents, don't let your child think that you think that he or she is not good enough, tell them hundreds of times a day that they are more than enough!

My lovely parents, don't let your child think that she or he is at fault for something that happened to you, be a real parent and take responsibility for your actions.

My lovely parents, don't let your child think that you think that she or he is not smart, tell them hundreds of times a day how smart they are.

And finally, my lovely parents, don't let your child think that you think that he or she is not beautiful and perfect just the way they are, tell them every single day hundreds of times how PRECIOUS and BEAUTIFUL THEY ARE.

THEY ARE OUR GIFTS FROM GOD!

And this explains the quote from Thomas Cooley with which we opened our journey, my lovely parents;

I AM NOT WHO YOU THINK I AM, I AM NOT WHO I THINK I AM,

I AM WHO I THINK YOU THINK I AM.

I think you think that we are done here, my lovely?

I don't think so☺. Until the next time.

With love,

your JD🙏

How can we create the life that we want to live? How can we find our true self?

How can we get rid of the ego MIND which keeps us stuck? How can we overcome our fears and our limited beliefs? These are the most common questions today, and the Author explains to us in simple terms based on his own experiences how to change the way we see ourselves and who we really are by changing the view of the world around us. And most importantly, our image of ourselves will also change, and we will be able to see through the eyes of possibilities, not problems, through the eyes of happiness, not worry, through the eyes of love, not fear, through the eyes of GOD, not EGO, through the eyes of ONENESS.

About the author

Jane was born in Kriva Palanka in Macedonia 37 years ago.

He finished his primary and high school in his home town with very good grades.

He graduated from the State University sv.Kiril and metodij in Skopje in the subject of Philosophy.

He didn't know that philosophy would open his mind and prepare him for what was awaiting him, for his true calling, to find the truth in himself and to share it FEARLESSLY with the world.

The truth about ONENESS.

He lives in Vienna Austria, he is married and he is a Father of three beautiful children, and they are his inspiration to make something of his life. To leave a trace of his existence.

To make them proud of their Dad one day, because he is already proud of them.

He knows DEEP INSIDE that one day they will make a big difference in the world by helping others and being loving human beings, just as they are NOW.

Sources

COVERSATIONS WITH GOD, Neale Donald Walsch

AWAKEN THE SPECIES, Neale Donald Walsch

YOU ARE THE UNIVERSE, Deepak Chopra, m.d

THE FEAR Kosta Petrov

BECOMING SUPERNATURAL Dr. Joe Dispenza

THE THIRD JESUS, Deepak Chopra, m.d

THE SEVEN SPIRITUAL LAWS OF SUCCESS, Deepak Chopra, m.d

THE IMPERSONAL LIFE Joseph Benner

THE BOOK OF SECRETS, Deepak Chopra, m.d

THE POWER OF NOW Eckhart Tolle

THE POWER OF AWAKENING, Dr. Wayne Dyer

GOD, A STORY OF REVELATION, Deepak Chopra, m.d

ZERO LIMITS Joe Vitale

POWER OF AWARENESS Neville Goddard

A big Thanks to the all great teachings of Morry Lefkoe, Michael Beckwith and Steve Harvey from the bottom of my heart.

Printed in the United States
by Baker & Taylor Publisher Services